Editor's Note

Jonathan Wilson, Editor

Over the past few months it had become common for football writers to refer to next summer's European Championship in France as "the last great tournament". Fans, readers and viewers won't have much sympathy, but when you're away from home for a month, working 12-hour days as standard seven days a week, there's consolation in manageable distances between stadiums, the ready availability of great food and booze and of being in a country whose culture you pretty much get.

Russia and Qatar, assuming they do go ahead, will be tough – for differing reasons. Euro 2020, with its multiple venues scattered across the continent, won't have the same feel. We were looking forward to France 2016. Then came the massacres in Paris on November 19. Even if Isis don't try anything in France next summer, it will be a very different tournament now, with a ramped up security presence and almost certain false alarms. I was at Slovenia's qualifying play-off against Ukraine the Tuesday after the attacks. Early in the game, somebody set off a firecracker and you saw the whole stand flinch. Moods can change quickly, but France 2016 will not, as we'd hoped, be a tournament of wine and cheese but of tension and anxiety.

In the wider scheme of things, of course the fact that a football tournament may not be as much fun as it should have been ranks pretty low when considering the impact of Isis. I doubt I was the only person who felt a little uncomfortable at the way football thrust itself front and centre after the attacks (at least I think it did; maybe it just felt like that because I read so much football media).

But then this was the first time there'd been a terrorist attack on a major football match (or at least one that hadn't been stifled early in the planning stage). And given how many people go to watch football each week, that does make it a major issue. As after the tube bombings in 2005, my first thought was to wonder how it hadn't happened earlier. These are the softest of targets. Even if you search everybody going into a ground, it would be easy enough to attack crowds on their way to or from a stadium. Which is, of course precisely what makes it so terrifying.

There was at least some of the usual snideness and cynicism before the England v France friendly and I confess I had my doubts about certain aspects of the memorials. I wasn't at Wembley – I was in Maribor – but the reaction dispelled them. The gratitude from the French public for English solidarity seemed heartfelt and for some there appeared genuine catharsis. Just as football can claim for itself too great a significance, it's important not to go too far the other way: symbolic moments can still have a power and that friendly, perhaps, was at least a sign that something approaching normality could still be achieved.

But there is more than symbolism to football's value. Maribor was the third game I'd seen in five days. I was in Zenica for Bosnia against Ireland and in Budapest for Hungary against Norway. Across those days I ate, drank and chatted with an array of journalists and other friends: English, Irish, Bosnian, Hungarian, Norwegian, Slovenian and Ukrainian. These are people I'd never have met had it not been for football, people with whom I'd have had little in common but for football, and people whose cultures I understand better and respect more because of football.

It provides anecdotes that will keep us entertained into our dotage: nobody who was in Zenica will forget the Irish journalist who, accidentally, hit a former Bosnia rugby international over the head with a chair, the Bosnian's anger or the Irishman's increasingly exasperated apologies, prompting the ritual retelling of the anecdote from Italia '90 about the Irish physio Mick Byrne inadvertently smashing a galleon made of matchsticks in a hotel lobby, seeing his apologies rebuffed by the hotel manager and eventually snapping, "I'm not fucking sorry any more. Fuck you and fuck your boat." Football itself is almost irrelevant in that: it is simply the currency in which the transaction

is made, but it seems to me those transactions are hugely valuable.

I then went on to Belgrade when I interviewed Vladica Popović and Dragoslav Šekularac, both of whom were in the Crvena Zvezda team that drew 3-3 with Manchester United in their final game before the Munich air crash. Šekularac had become friends with Bobby Charlton and recalled fondly taking him to the bar in the Hotel Metropol where he got a discount. When United returned to Belgrade in 1966 to play Partizan in the European Cup semi-final, Popović sought out Harry Gregg to wish him well. Perhaps for no better reason than that football is such a simple game, it facilitates such exchanges. (Of course, as hooliganism, social media and the comments sections show, it can also be a stage for stupidity, violence and general prickishness.)

And that it can be a global medium for the exchanges of views sets it in direct opposition to Isis and its determination to impose on the world its own restrictive vision.

The Blizzard has started a series of podcasts, essentially a series of audio versions of some of our best articles. They can be downloaded from the *www.theblizzard.co.uk* or via iTunes.

Contents

The Blizzard, Issue Nineteen

GOALS ARE OVERRATED...
THE BEAUTY IS IN THE STRUGGLE.

Exclusively available online from **www.theblizzard.co.uk** and **www.goalsoul.net**

THE BLIZZARD BY GOALSOUL
A PARTNERSHIP BORN OF FOOTBALL

In celebration of our most popular design, The Blizzard and goalsoul have decided to release 'Goals are overrated...' across three stunning new colour combinations.

The Blizzard by goalsoul partnership is a commitment to style and substance in equal measure. Our stunning and original graphic tees look and feel great. Lovingly hand screen-printed on 100% combed-cotton and shrink-resistant fabric — you can be sure of the highest possible quality, durability and wearability.

10

Mourinho

"The more the ball circulates in midfield,
the more likely it is that the other team
will dispossess us"

The Devil's Party

The manager, his methods and why it always goes wrong in the third season.

By Jonathan Wilson

At the beginning of May 2015, Chelsea wrapped up the Premier League title with a scrappy 1-0 win over Crystal Palace. It was not a great game or a great performance, but then for a couple of months Chelsea had looked exhausted, dragging their fatigued limbs over the line and grateful no contender was able to make a serious or consistent challenge. It was a day of relief as well as exultation, Mourinho's third title with the club, his first since his return and only the fifth they had ever won, despite all their recent investment.

Nobody then, perhaps, realised quite what a struggle those final yards had been, had any notion just how difficult things had become. Certainly nobody suspected then what would happen this season as Chelsea suffered the worst opening third to a campaign of any defending champion – worse than Leeds United, who finished seventeenth in 1992-93, worse even than Manchester City, who were relegated in 1937-38. Nobody recognised that what we were seeing was not necessarily a weary champion staggering to the finish but a club entering a period of profound crisis.

Mourinho's mood, too, was strange. He could have been forgiven for seeming jaded, yet his mood in the post-match press conference was neither tired nor celebratory. Usually such end-of-season events are relaxed affairs: "Tell us how you won", "Who was the most important player?", "Which game was key?" and, perhaps, if somebody is feeling especially mischievous and isn't just writing the same reflective piece as everybody else, "How can you be even greater next season?"

But Mourinho was as chippy as ever. This day of joy, he decided, was the perfect time for delivering another thrust in his on-going feud with Pep Guardiola. "For me," he said, "I'm not the smartest guy to choose countries and clubs. I could choose another club in another country where to be champion is easier." He didn't name Guardiola, but the reference was clear. Guardiola had gone to a super-club where the question is less "Who will win the title?" than "How many will Bayern win it by?" His titles, Mourinho was suggesting, meant less than the one he had just won. To some extent he was right, of course, and if he'd been making a general critique of the iniquities of global football finance, he might even have come across as statesmanlike, but his point was limited to Guardiola and his personal antipathy.

"I choose a club where I was happier before and a country where you are happy before," he went on. "I took a risk. I am so, so happy because I won another

Premier League title 10 years after [my first] in my second spell at the club. I was champion at every club I coached. I came to Inter, Real Madrid and Chelsea. Every title is important, to win the title in Spain with 100 points against the best Barcelona ever was a big achievement that I enjoyed so much. Maybe in the future I have to be smarter and choose another club in another country where everybody is champion. Maybe I will go to a country where a kitman can be coach and win the title. Maybe I need to be smarter but I still enjoy these difficulties. I think I'm at the right place. I'm here until [the Chelsea owner Roman] Abramovich tells me to go."

Even by Mourinho's standards, this was weird. Why would anybody, having just lifted the title, choose to belittle their rival, a rival who operates in another country? And not just a passing jibe, an under-the-breath aside, but a full-on assault. Mourinho could have criticised Guardiola by implication, by pointing out he had come back to Chelsea for love, by outlining the difficulties he had faced, by paying tribute to the competitiveness of the Premier League, but instead he chose to sneer. In the moment of his triumph, Mourinho chose to make the conversation about Guardiola.

In hindsight, that final sentence seems strange too: here until Abramovich tells him to go? Mourinho had said on his return to Chelsea that he wanted to found a dynasty, that in a career laden with silverware that was something he still hadn't done and yet that line, seemingly so throwaway, hinted at an insecurity. Perhaps it was merely part of his contract negotiations: he did, after all, sign a new four-year deal a few weeks later.

Odd as the attack on Guardiola was, it followed a pattern. Increasingly, as the season had gone on, it had become apparent that Mourinho is obsessed by Barcelona and, specifically, by Guardiola as the manifestation of the Barcelona philosophy. He was once among them, but they rejected him. He once worked with Louis van Gaal at a time when the club was home to the men who would shape modern coaching.

Mourinho left to make his fortune and succeeded, but when he wanted to return they denied him. He was a little bit different. He wasn't a player but a translator-turned-coach. He wasn't one of them. He didn't think like them. He didn't instantly revere Rinus Michels. He looked at the game and asked not how to win while playing well, but simply how to win. He had a pragmatic edge that meant he never quite fitted in. He came, in 2008, replete with honours, wanting to be coach and they preferred one of their own, whose coaching experience consisted of one season with the reserve team. He became the outcast, the rebel, the fallen angel. He began to define himself in opposition to Barcelona and thus to the prevailing footballing ethos of the age, determining, like Satan in *Paradise Lost*, that "glory never shall his wrath or might extort from me." He would not play by their rules; he do things his way in self-conscious opposition and prove that he was right. He vowed, like Milton's Satan, "to wage by force of guile eternal war, irreconcilable to our grand Foe."

When Van Gaal arrived at Barça in 1997, it was supposed to be as the club's youth co-ordinator, but he was soon asked to take over as manager as Robson, despite winning both the Copa del Rey and the Cup-Winners' Cup, was shuffled into an ambassadorial role because of poor league form. On Robson's recommendation, Van Gaal took on Mourinho to be his "third assistant". At 34, it was a huge step for Mourinho, the first real sign that he was respected by figures at the top of the global game.

Mourinho had been born into football. His grandfather had been president of Vitória de Setúbal. His father had been a goalkeeper – he saved a penalty from Eusébio on the forward's debut – and then went into coaching. Mourinho wanted to be a player but after spells at Rio Ave, where his father was coach, Belenense and Sesimbra, he recognised that coaching offered him a more promising future. His father's career helped make him aware what an ungrateful world football can be: Mourinho has often referred to one Christmas when he was "nine or ten" when his father was sacked on Christmas Day. Actually, it happened in 1984 when Mourinho was 21, but the general point remains: no matter what you've done in the past – Mourinho Snr had taken Rio Ave to promotion and a Portuguese Cup final – a run of bad results can bring the end.

Mourinho Jnr became a student at the Instituto Superior de Educação Física in Lisbon and came under the influence of Professor Manuel Sérgio, who believed that football knowledge was not enough, that a coach also had to be a psychologist, a public speaker and have a grasp of the sciences. In 1987, Mourinho left the college and worked for a while as a PE teacher at various primary schools, specialising in helping children with disabilities.

From being a teenager, Mourinho had helped his father, preparing scouting reports on opponents – perhaps significantly, looking for ways their way of playing could be hampered. Vitoria de Setúbal, a club where his father had played and coached, took him on as a youth team coach. He fulfilled the same role at Estrela de Amadora and then became a scout at Ovarense. Eventually, in 1992, he got his big break, appointed to work with Robson at Sporting.

Robson, a naturally open and garrulous man, took to discussing tactics with Mourinho and, as they moved to Porto and then Barcelona, gave him more and more responsibility, getting him to plan training sessions and prepare dossiers on opponents, recognising that the younger man's meticulousness and natural caution were a useful counter-balance to his own spontaneity and attacking instincts.

Barcelona in the mid-nineties was an extraordinary place to be, not just because they won the league two seasons running, but because of the people who were there. Guardiola and Luis Enrique were already together in midfield when Van Gaal took over. Julen Lopetegui, a back-up goalkeeper, and Laurent Blanc departed as Van Gaal arrived. A year later, Phillip Cocu joined the midfield and Ronald Koeman arrived as an assistant coach. Frank de Boer was signed the year after that. In Mourinho's time at the club, Barça were home not only to the Chelsea manager, but also the current managers of Bayern, Barça, Manchester United, Porto, PSV and Southampton. They are not clones of each other, but it was at the Camp Nou in the late 90s that the prevailing ethos of modern football was formed.

The predominant style, of course, was that which has sustained Barcelona since the days of Vic Buckingham, Rinus Michels and Johan Cruyff (the player) in the early seventies: they were the ideas of Ajax, Total Football, a belief in possession football, rooted in a high offside line, pressing and the interchange of players on the field. Cruyff as manager reinforced this and, although he saw Van Gaal's version of the game as overly mechanised, the starting point was the same. This was perhaps the greatest coaching seminar in history, and the philosophy it taught was that which had been flowing from Ajax to Barcelona, which believed the same things but had more money, for three decades: what we might perhaps term Barçajax school. Even Robson had played under Buckingham at West Bromwich Albion.

Not that anybody remarked upon it then, but Mourinho was an outsider looking in. He hadn't played at Ajax or Barcelona – or even West Brom – so although much of his experience at the top end of football had been under Barçajax thinkers, those ideals perhaps weren't as deeply ingrained in him as they were in others. Van Gaal was impressed by his work on positional play and allowed him to give tactical advice at half-time and to coach the team in friendlies. As he became increasingly confident, Van Gaal found "an arrogant young man, who didn't respect authority that much, but I did like that of him. He was not submissive, used to contradict me when he thought I was in the wrong. Finally I wanted to hear what he had to say and ended up listening to him more than the rest of my assistants."

Barcelona was Mourinho's education. The next stage was to put it into practice. Mourinho left Barcelona to take up the assistant manager's job at Benfica in the summer of 2000, recognising that it was at home that he was most likely to get an opportunity. Sure enough, four games into the season Jupp Heynckes left the club and Mourinho stepped up to replace him. His reign lasted only nine games: Mourinho resigned after the new club president Manuel Vilharino indicated that he wanted to give the manager's job to the former Benfica defender Toni.

Mourinho was appointed coach of União de Leiria in July 2001. They are a small club and their budget was extremely limited, but playing hard-nosed counter-attacking footbal Mourinho had them third by January. They fell away towards the end of the season but Portugal's big clubs had taken note and, the following January, Mourinho was appointed manager of Porto, replacing Octavio Machado.

It was at Porto that Mourinho's ideas were first tested on a stage he saw as befitting his talents. It was there that he first achieved the sort of control over a side that he demanded, there that he was competing for titles rather than scrapping to avoid relegation. That allowed him to be more expansive in his approach. "At Porto he practised attacking football, but in Italy he played differently, because he didn't have a team that gave him the same guarantees offensively speaking," said the centre-back Jorge Costa, the captain of that side, who was recalled by Mourinho from a loan spell at Charlton Athletic. "I think it's a huge mistake to say a coach is either offensive or defensive, because we should always coach according to the reality we are inserted in. Mourinho is a great example of that. He didn't separate offence from defence, instead he worked the tactic as one."

Even at Porto, though, there were limits to how much freedom Mourinho was prepared to give players. "He didn't let me or any of the other centre-backs go up the pitch with the ball," said Costa. "I did it sometimes and he hated it, clearly letting me know later that this would unbalance the team. He would allow the full-backs to go up but that would always be compensated by one of the midfielders."

At Porto, Mourinho tended to favour a 4-3-3 in the league, switching to a 4-4-2 with a diamond in midfield for the Champions League. For Jorge Costa, though, that was not a sign of reactivity; it wasn't that Mourinho's principal aim became to stop the opposition playing. "He never changed tactics thinking about the opponents, but always thinking about us, about his own side," he said. "He changed so we could play along with his strategy. We would always stick to our tactics, the 4-3-3 or the 4-4-2 diamond, but those formations didn't mean we had to be offensive or defensive: it depended on the match, it depended on what he wanted us to do on each night. More than formations, our team lived off its dynamic, because despite changing formations we would never change our playing philosophy."

In the Champions League campaign. Mourinho's midfield comprised Costinha holding, with Maniche to the right, Dmitri Aleinichev to the left, and Deco creating behind a front two of Carlos Alberto and Derlei. Attacking width came from Paulo Ferreira and Nuno Valente pushing forward from full-back. "I didn't like the 4-4-2 diamond that much," said Maniche, "because I didn't touch the ball so often. In that formation the midfielders at the sides of the diamond needed to cover for the left- and right-backs, who went forward a lot."

The shape, though, was a minor detail alongside the style. "He wanted us to press very high," said Maniche. "He wanted the team to react quickly when they lose the ball, so we gain it in their midfield. This pressure would be done as a team, and not only one or two players. He would prepare us for each game throughout the week and work on that. If he knew that one of the central defenders had trouble on the ball, he would tell us to pressure the other defender, to force the weaker one to run with the ball. It depended a bit on whom we were facing; he liked to have possession as well."

That, of course is the essence of the Barçajax school: pressing and possessing. But Porto also had their own style. Mourinho was heavily influenced by his director of methodology, Victor Frade, one of the pioneers of periodisation, who preferred the low block, sitting deep and absorbing pressure. Porto tended to press, but they could also drop off. Most importantly, possession was never fetishised: "The more the ball circulates in midfield," Mourinho said, "the more likely it is that the other team will dispossess us." That was the first expression of a theory that would later become notorious.

So while it would be misleading to suggest that Porto played the Barçajax way, it wasn't too far removed from what had been going on at the Camp Nou the previous decade. Nor was his use of the goalkeeper Vítor Baía, who rates Mourinho as the best coach he worked under. "I was very important in the defensive organisation and also in the first moment of transition," he said. "Mourinho liked the Dutch style, which meant the keeper had to know how to play with his feet, had to know how to start an attack. Our defensive line was mid-high on the pitch, so that tells you a lot about how we pressed, very high. This obviously was good for me, because I was more involved in the game: I loved to initiate attacks and be a part of the switching of the ball from one side to the other."

Yet for all players from that Porto side insist Mourinho didn't change for specific matches, he would present them with dossiers on their opponents. "One of the most important aspects about José, which I support, is that the other team has to be the one making the changes, you have to keep your own identity," said Costinha. "Of course, he would give us detailed information about the team we were facing next at the start of the training week and more precisely about the player that would be closest to our area of play. 'What was the player like? Did he have a tendency to get many cards? What kind of movements did he make?' It was new for many of us back then, but it was very helpful and meant we were much better prepared for each match."

Where Mourinho excelled was in his attention to detail and, specifically, in anticipating scenarios that might occur during the game. "Those things happened all the time," said Vítor Baía. "Sometimes it was as though he could see the future. I remember a specific incident against Benfica, when throughout the week he prepared us for what we should do after we scored a goal... He told us that [the Benfica coach José Antonio] Camacho would make a specific substitution and change his tactics, which was what happened. So we already knew what to do when he did it; we were completely prepared for it. For the same match, we also prepared to play with 10 players, because José knew the referee would not be able to take the pressure and would show a red card along the way. That also happened, but we had already seen that movie during the week, so we knew what to do and got a narrow win."

Mourinho still readies his side for different scenarios today. When Chelsea beat PSG 2-0 in the Champions League in 2014, for instance, to go through on away goals, John Terry revealed that they'd practised for various different scorelines, even down to the system with three centre-forwards plus André Schürrle plus Willian they used for the final 10 minutes as they chased the vital second goal. Specific preparation is key; as little as possible is left to chance.

Mourinho's other way of preparing for big games, was psychological. "The rivalries would do their work," Maniche said, "and the press conferences." An ability to play the media has always been a Mourinho strength, antagonising opponents and pressuring referees. The flip side of that is his relationship with his own squad, a capacity to create remarkably strong bonds.

That, perhaps, is an aspect of Mourinho that is often overlooked, that while he can be grouchy with the media, while he pursues feuds with rivals and can fall out with his own players, he is also capable of inspiring devotion. There are stories of players in tears as he hugged them goodbye on his first departure from Chelsea. "He would fool around with us outside practice, but when the time to work arrived he would be ruthless," said Vítor Baía. "We only practised for one hour each day, yet those hours were the most intense I've ever seen."

The goalkeeper stresses how good Mourinho was at handling different personalities, what an astute man-manager he was. "He knew everybody so deeply that he could control our emotions in every situation," he said. "In my case, he would just pat me on the back and I was ready to go. However, there were players who needed motivation, who needed to be praised, and he knew which ones needed what, that's what made him so good."

That, though, is not quite the full story, which explains much about Mourinho's Machiavellian charm, the sense he gives of planning out every interaction. In September 2002, Vítor Baía was banned from all club activities for a month after a training-ground row with Mourinho. "That was the turning point in his career," Vítor Baía said. "He was very young and wanted to make a statement – and he did it. We had a great relationship, because we had been together at Porto with Bobby Robson, then for three years in Barcelona, with him always as assistant coach, but when he arrived at Porto he wanted to show everyone who was the boss: friends off the pitch, players on it. Performance was what counted, not relationships, so I was not in the best

form and was chosen as an example: I was his statement. Of course I was not pleased at the time. Today, after many conversations with him and the assistant coaches from the time and some players, I know that it was all a plan. Everyone knew how to react to me, how to speak to me, everyone was ready. After the month of suspension José welcomed me back with a big hug and I was straight back into the first team."

Porto won the league that season with a record points tally and also claimed both the Portuguese Cup and the Uefa Cup, their approach in the final infuriating the Celtic manager Martin O'Neill, who accused them of diving, feigning injury and time-wasting. They defended the league title the following season and also added the Champions League. Mourinho made another step up and was appointed manager of Chelsea.

Given the rush of success that followed, given how Mourinho charmed English football in his first season, it's easy to forget now that his first weeks at Chelsea were faltering – at least from a tactical point of view. Initially, Mourinho used the midfield diamond he'd deployed with Porto in the Champions League. In his first match, a hard-fought 1-0 win over Manchester United, Claude Makelele patrolled in front of the back four, while Frank Lampard was deployed behind a front two of Didier Drogba and Eiður Guðjohnsen with Geremi and Alexei Smertin at the sides of the diamond. Joe Cole and Thiago Mendes sometimes came in as the flanking players and Mateja Kežman sometimes played instead of Guðjohnsen, but that was the shape for the first six league games of the season. Chelsea conceded only one goal in that spell and picked up 14 points, but they only scored six goals. Lampard seemed uneasy as a number 10, struggling to play with his back to goal and lacking the tight technical skills or vision to operate as Deco had for Porto. Mourinho spoke about the importance of practising not only attacking and defending but also the transitions from attack to defence and defence to attack, and introduced to public consciousness the concept of "resting on the ball", passing it around at the back to give players time to recuperate, but his football was scratchy and, frankly, a little dull.

Against Middlesbrough in September 2004, though, he changed shape to the 4-3-3 that became characteristic of that period at Chelsea. Damian Duff came in on the left with Guðjohnsen pushing across to the right, while Lampard fell back into a shuttling midfield role in which he excelled, specialising in those late runs into the box that brought him 13 goals that season. Remorselessly, relentlessly, Chelsea swept to the title. There were a couple of dabbles with a back three, and Arjen Robben sometimes played on the wing, but the 4-3-3 was the base.

Mourinho was more cautious than he had been at Porto, most notably in the way the full-backs – Paulo Ferreira and Wayne Bridge in that first season – rarely advanced beyond the halfway line. His side didn't press anywhere near as high, in part because of the lack of pace of John Terry at centre-back. The shift away from the Barçajax model had begun. Chelsea conceded only 15 goals while amassing 95 points in 38 games, both Premier League records.

The only problem was the suspicion that Roman Abramovich felt that having invested as much as he had, he might be due a little more entertainment. Hernán Crespo, Michael Essien and Shaun Wright-Phillips arrived that summer and there were experiments with a front two again in the first two games of the season, against Wigan and Arsenal, both won 1-0. But the 4-3-3 soon returned and so did the sense of Chelsea as a remorseless winning machine. They conceded seven goals more and won four points fewer, but they still took the title by eight points from Manchester United.

But the whispers about Abramovich's dissatisfaction were growing ever stronger. He had decided to buy a football club after watching Manchester United's 4-3 victory over Real Madrid at Old Trafford in March 2003: football like that was what he wanted (although his excitement at that game in particular perhaps suggests his lack of understanding: Real Madrid were 3-1 up from the first leg and never in serious danger). So he bought more stars: Andriy Shevchenko arrived, and so did Ashley Cole, Michael Ballack, Salomon Kalou and, after a protracted tussle with United, Mikel John Obi.

Mourinho was unimpressed. There were awkward attempts to squeeze Shevchenko into a 4-4-2, or to play a narrow 4-3-3 with Shevchenko on the flank, but none really worked. Shevchenko, who had just turned 30, never seemed to have recovered fully from a knee injury from which he had rushed back to play in the World Cup; there were times when Mourinho seemed openly to despair of his form, laughing ruefully at another bungled first touch. Chelsea were still essentially defensively solid, but they lacked anything approaching fluency. They only lost three times that season but, ending it with five successive draws, they surrendered the title to United having scored 19 goals fewer than the champions.

The relationship between Mourinho and Abramovich soured as the season went on, reaching crisis point in a League Cup semi-final first leg at Wycombe. Injuries meant Chelsea fielded Essien and Paulo Ferreira at centre-back and, after a 1-1 draw against the League Two side, Mourinho erupted. In a small room off the tunnel at Adams Park, as a tea urn belched steam into the freezing January air, he bemoaned, in his characteristically sulky way, a recruitment policy that had left him overburdened with attacking players but bereft of defensive cover. It was a mesmerising incident, partly because of the incongruity of the sophisticated manager and the parochial surroundings and partly because the player Mourinho was so desperate to sign was Tal Ben Haim. The Israel international did arrive that summer and played just 13 league games before being offloaded.

Mourinho lingered a further eight months after the rant in the steam, but as Abramovich appointed Avram Grant as technical director, the atmosphere became increasingly rancorous and, in September 2007, after following up a 2-0 defeat at Aston Villa with a 0-0 draw at home to Blackburn, he was gone.

Soon after Mourinho had left Chelsea, it became apparent that Frank Rijkaard's

time at Barcelona was coming to an end. "A 5% drop in commitment at the highest level creates difficulty," the then Barcelona CEO Ferran Soriano wrote in his book *Goal: The Ball Doesn't Go in by Chance*, "and Frank didn't know how to re-energise the group." Barça considered appointing Mourinho in January 2008, but decided that Rijkaard should be allowed to complete the season so the new manager was coming in afresh.

Txiki Begiristain, Barça's technical director, interviewed Mourinho, telling him that the final decision would be taken by Johan Cruyff, who held no official position but who, as the living embodiment of the Barçajax ethos, had an authority that transcended the club's politics. Mourinho, determined to press his case, called the club president Joan Laporta and asked to speak to Cruyff. Laporta replied that the decision had already been taken: Barça were going to appoint Pep Guardiola. Mourinho told Laporta he'd made a terrible mistake.

Soriano explained that the club had set out nine criteria by which prospective candidates were judged:

1. Respect for the sports-management model and the role of the technical director

2. Playing style

3. Promoting the right values in the first team and paying special attention to the development of young talent

4. Training and performance

5. Proactive management of the dressing-room

6. Other responsibilities with, and commitment to, the club, including maintaining a conservative profile and avoiding overuse of the media

7. Experience as a player and a coach at the highest level

8. Support for the good governance of the club

9. Knowledge of the Spanish league, the club and European competition.

According to Soriano, the decision came down to a straight head-to-head between Mourinho and Guardiola. Both fell down on point nine, but Mourinho also fell down on points two, three, six and eight. "It was clear that Mourinho was a great coach but we thought Guardiola would be even better," said Soriano. "There was the important issue of knowledge of the club. Mourinho had it, but Guardiola had more of it and he enjoyed a greater affinity with the club. Mourinho is a winner, but in order to win he guarantees a level of tension that becomes a problem."

Mourinho has never forgiven Barcelona.

In the summer of 2008, Mourinho joined Inter. As at Chelsea, he found a team that lacked pace in the heart of its defence and so sat his back four deep, although the full-backs, Maxwell and Maicon, were given some licence to push on. The shape at the front changed fairly regularly, but the most common system was a 4-3-1-2, with Esteban Cambiasso flanked by the industrious Javier Zanetti and Sulley Muntari, with Dejan Stankovic

creating behind Zlatan Ibrahimović and one of his many partners. Inter lost just four times in winning the league by 10 points — their fourth successive title. The following season was tighter, with the title won by just two points, but that year also brought the Champions League — Inter's first in 45 years.

The final, a 2-0 win on Madrid over Van Gaal's Bayern, was straightforward enough, but the symbolism of Mourinho overcoming his former boss was overshadowed by the far greater resonance of the semi-final in April 2010, and Inter's extraordinary backs to the wall triumph over Guardiola's Barcelona, the defending champions. Mourinho had the great good fortune, of course, that the eruption of Eyjafjallajökull meant that Barça had to travel to Milan by bus, which perhaps partly explained their sluggish performance in losing 3-1. Inter lined up in a 4-2-3-1, with Cambiasso partnered by Thiago Motta at the back of midfield. Samuel Eto'o, Wesley Sneijder and Goran Pandev offered creativity behind Diego Milito, but what was noticeable was how quickly they could drop back to form a five-man midfield. Milito's aerial ability then gave Inter an outlet.

But it was at the Camp Nou that Mourinho had his revenge on Barcelona and Guardiola. Motta was sent off after 29 minutes thanks to Sergio Busquets's playacting, at which Inter went even more defensive than they had been previously, dropping all nine outfielders who remained behind the ball and at times seemingly deliberately giving away possession so as not to lose their defensive shape. Eto'o and Cristian Chivu, who came in for Pandev, ended up effectively playing as auxiliary full-backs. Again and again Barça swept forward and again and again they found the low block waiting for them, an impenetrable mass of white shirts that denied them the space for their rat-a-tat flurries of passing.

Inter had one shot to Barcelona's 15 and just 19% possession, but they held out for a one-goal defeat and an aggregate victory; in so they doing struck a blow against Barça and all they stood for, in their own stadium. When Barça turned on the sprinklers as the Inter players celebrated, Mourinho must have been even more delighted: he hadn't just won, he'd provoked Barça into an act of pettiness and so helped dislodge their halo.

Inter only ever seemed like a stepping-stone. While his time there helped reinforce parallels with Helenio Herrera, the high priest of *catenaccio* who had won two European Cups in the sixties, the sense was always that Mourinho was eyeing a return to either England or Spain. That's where the money was and that's where the real power was – which of course made the fact he has won Champions Leagues with clubs from outside the very elite all the more impressive. And, perhaps most importantly, Spain was where Barcelona and Guardiola were.

Real Madrid had been in contact with Mourinho since 2007, when they'd signed Pepe, a fellow client of the super-agent Jorge Mendes. Manuel Pellegrini had never had the full support of the board and, as his reign drifted to its conclusion, Inter's victory over Barcelona suggested Mourinho was the man who

could topple Guardiola's side. Such was the desperation to bring his empire down that the quibbles that had existed in the mind of the president Florentino Pérez over Mourinho's style of play were pushed to one side. They appointed him in summer 2010.

Mourinho started out with a 4-2-3-1 with Xabi Alonso alongside Sami Khedira at the back of midfield, then Cristiano Ronaldo, Mesut Özil and Ángel Di María behind Gonzalo Higuaín. There were goalless draws away to Mallorca and Levante, but when Madrid went to the Camp Nou on November 29, they were a point clear at the top. This was the moment Madrid had been waiting for, the moment when Mourinho was supposed to show he could bring down Guardiola.

His plan was to do what he had done seven months earlier, to operate a low block and look to frustrate Barça. The previous season, though, Bara had had Ibrahimović up front: their front three of Pedro, Messi and David Villa presented a different, more mobile treat. Within 14 minutes, Barça were 2-0 up. Mourinho switched to a high press and then at half-time brought on Lassana Diarra for Özil, the first sighting of what became known as the "*trivote*" of Diarra, Khedira and Xabi Alonso – the term suggesting three *pivotes*, or holding players. It didn't work, and Barça won 5-0.

Madrid only lost another three games that season, but that wasn't enough. Barça took not only the league title but also the Champions League, beating Madrid in the semi-final. The *trivote* was seen more and more against high-class opposition, despite opposition form various players – or at least that's what Diego Torres claimed in his controversial biography of Mourinho. The book is clearly written from a highly critical perspective, but equally clearly it was written from excellent — if partisan — sources within the dressing room. He suggests that Mourinho at Madrid was not motivated merely by winning — which had been almost his sole objective elsewhere — but by the desire to do so in his way, to establish himself as a tactical pioneer. Mourinho spoke repeatedly of the *trivote*, his triangle of aggressive, hard-tackling midfielders who could press high and, in theory, either win the ball back high up the pitch or offer an impenetrable block in front of the back four. What was baffling to Torres's sources was partly that Mourinho seemed to portray himself as the inventor of the system when the term had been coined by Santiago Segurola in *El País* during the 1998 World Cup to describe Italy's midfield three of Dino Baggio, Luigi Di Biagio and Gianluca Pesotto. More worrying was that he played it at times when, as the sources saw it, it was of limited benefit and meant playing players out of position. It was as though, the implication was, he was determined above all else to promote his own legend. Maybe that's true, maybe it isn't — Torres's book isn't the most disinterested source — but what is true is that Mourinho's record in big games as Real Madrid coach, particularly away from home, was poor.

In the first (home) leg of semi-final against Barça, Mourinho fielded a *trivote* of Diarra, Xabi Alonso and Pepe, who was, predictably, sent off. Messi then scored twice as Barça won 2-0 on thir way to a 3-1 aggregate triumph. The whole tie was played out in a sulphurous atmosphere, largely of Mourinho's making. Madrid did little but spoil: even if Barça did dive and whinge, at its heart the rivalry had become about one team passing and dribbling, the other kicking and brawling; light against dark, football against anti-football. In the 17 *Clásicos* Mourinho was involved in in his time as Madrid manager, his side committed 346 fouls to Barcelona's 220.

According to Torres, Mourinho laid out a simple seven-point plan for winning big games:

1. The game is won by the team who commits fewer errors.

2. Football favours whoever provokes more errors in the opposition.

3. Away from home, instead of trying to be superior to the opposition, it's better to encourage their mistakes.

4. Whoever has the ball is more likely to make a mistake.

5. Whoever renounces possession reduces the possibility of making a mistake.

6. Whoever has the ball has fear.

7. Whoever does not have it is thereby stronger.

This is the antithesis of the Barçajax approach, a categorical rejection of the possession-based, proactive approach of Guardiola and his ilk. It was precisely how Inter had played in that Champions League semi-final but there was always a sense at Madrid that it was somehow unworthy of the club.

The only comfort came in the Copa del Rey as Madrid beat Barça 1-0 in the final; perhaps Barça were not invincible, perhaps Madrid could get under their skin. The bitterness carried over into the following season, and Barça meeting Madrid over two legs for the Super Cup. A 2-2 draw at the Bernabéu was followed by a 3-2 win for Barça at the Camp Nou, the winner scored by Messi with two minutes remaining. Marcelo was then sent off in injury time for a lunge on Cesc Fàbregas and in the brawl that followed Özil was red-carded and Mourinho poked Tito Vilanova, the Barça assistant coach in the eye from behind. It was an act of cowardice and petulance that would have profound consequences.

Still, in the short term, Madrid did break Barça's stranglehold on the league. Playing a 4-2-3-1 for most of the 2011-12 campaign, Madrid lost just twice and finished nine points above a weary Barça. Their Champions League run was ended by Bayern on penalties in the semi-final. Guardiola, exhausted, left at the end of the season and the way seemed clear for Madrid to create their own empire.

But 2012-13 began abysmally as Madrid took just four points from their opening four games, beaten by Getafe and Sevilla. By the time they lost 1-0 at Granada in early February, the season was over and the title was Barcelona's, despite Gerardo Martino's struggles as manager. Players complained – as they had done in the previous two seasons — that too much time was spent practising the counter-attack and very little practising against massed defences. The Champions League brought a humbling semi-final defeat to Borussia Dortmund, who seemed quicker, sharper, better at the counter-attack that was supposed to be Mourinho's strong point.

On 7 May 2013, Mourinho arrived alone at the Sheraton Madrid Mirasierra to prepare for a league game against Malaga, having refused to travel with his players after accusing them of disloyalty. A contingent of the Ultras Sur, who saw themselves as Madrid's most devoted fans, were waiting for him with a banner that proclaimed their love for him. There was effectively a state of open warfare between Mourinho and the club captain Iker Casillas. That Mourinho's fractious time at the club was coming to an end wasn't in any real doubt. And for Mourinho, things were about to get much worse.

That night, the story broke that Manchester United were going to appoint David Moyes as a successor to Alex Ferguson. According to Torres although he is contradicted by Ferguson, the Madrid manager was appalled. He'd believed he had a special relationship with Ferguson, but the outgoing United manager hadn't even called him to let him know of the decision. That night Mourinho was restless, fretful, constantly checking the news to see if there may have been some mistake. The following morning he called Jorge Mendes to see if it might be possible to derail the deal and reinsert himself into the picture. By the following day, Mourinho was insisting that his intention had always been to go back to Chelsea, that his wife wanted to live in London. Perhaps that was true, but perhaps he saw this as a second betrayal. Worse was the sense that this was a decision that was only indirectly related to football. "A United manager," Bobby Charlton, at the time a United director, told the *Guardian* in December 2012, "would not do what he did to Tito Vilanova... Mourinho is a really good coach, but that's as far as I'd go." And his behaviour at Madrid had raised other doubts. "The problem is," one executive at Gestifute , Mendes's agency, told Torres, "when things do not go well for Mou, he does not follow the club's line. He follows José's line."

By then, his options by then were limited: other than PSG, Chelsea was the only club of sufficient stature who would still have him. Not only that, but he was, at least, going back to a club where he'd been revered, where he'd announced himself as "a special one" and been loved for it, where the fans didn't seem to mind – perhaps even relished – his pragmatic approach (whether Abramovich was so keen on it was another matter).

In summer 2013, Mourinho arrived at Chelsea for a second time promising he had mellowed, that he was now "the happy one". With Oscar, Eden Hazard and one other (sometimes Kevin De Bruyne, sometimes Juan Mata, sometimes André Schürrle, sometimes Willian) operating behind a striker, there was even an attempt to play more spectacular football. That lasted until a League Cup quarter-final defeat at Sunderland in the December. Mourinho, looking tired and dishevelled, spoke after the game of going back to basics. He had nine days before Chelsea played again and when they did, they stifled Arsenal at the Emirates in an utterly tedious 0-0 draw. Mourinho afterwards seemed positively jolly. Chelsea conceded just four goals and went unbeaten through

the following 13 league games. Surprise defeats to Aston Villa, Crystal Palace and Sunderland derailed their title challenge but they still had an outside chance when they went to Liverpool for their fourth-last game of the season.

A draw would have kept Liverpool ahead of Manchester City, but Mourinho turned to his Madrid manual for big games. Chelsea spoiled and wasted time from the off, showed little interest in the ball, had 23% of possession and won because of a Steven Gerrard slip just before half-time and a late goal on the break from Willian, as though to validate the theory that if you wait long enough, the opponent will eventually make a mistake: "Whoever has the ball has fear."

The signing of Nemanja Matić in the January had given Chelsea extra solidity in midfield. Cesc Fàbregas and Diego Costa arrived in the summer, adding midfield guile and a tough, awkward, goalscoring leader of the line. From their opening game, a 3-1 win at Burnley, Chelsea looked like champions. They lost only three times all season, and one of those was after the championship had been wrapped up.

To those who have known him the longest, this was the same old Mourinho. "I didn't feel any difference when it came to communication with the players," said Maniche. "I recently did some work with Chelsea and some of the processes were the same when it came to training. The warm-up, for example, was practically the same I had in Porto."

Costinha insists that the fundamentals have remained constant throughout Mourinho's career. "I was lucky enough to see him work at Porto, Chelsea, Inter and a bit at Real Madrid, and the only thing that changed were the players," he said. "All the clubs were different, and what he did was to shape the players he had at each club to his philosophy after studying each one, after understanding how he could be useful to the team."

As City collapsed in January and Chelsea's progress to the title became more and more certain – even though they showed signs of fatigue – the focus shifted away from who would win and towards how a champion should play. Chelsea, better than any other side in England, could close down a game when they needed to and so the question began to be asked whether they were boring. "That question doesn't even make sense to me," said Jorge Costa, who is now manager of Gabon. "It's obvious the most important aspect of coaching is winning. I hated to lose when I was a player, and I still hate it as a coach. I really don't think there was a team playing better than Chelsea last season."

For Maniche, similarly, the question is simply naïve. "The ideal was to do what we did in Porto, which was win and play very well and attractively in practically every match," he said. "But football has changed completely and it will be completely different again in 10 years. Those critics have no idea of what football is, apparently. Arsenal seem to enjoy having a coach who does not win titles, but ask their fans if they wouldn't like Mourinho better, ask any team in the world if they would not have Moruinho as their coach. What would you prefer? Winning is not only part of the game, but it's also a part of your life. You need to win, and to win, you need Mourinho."

Mourinho himself is unapologetic about prioritising winning. "I don't think it's changed from one century ago... there is no kid, even playing with his cousin or his father, even in the garden, there is no kid that plays to lose," he said. "The nature, the sense of it – doesn't change. They play to win. I used to play a lot in my neighbourhood. And I don't remember it ever being any other than a big fight to win. I don't think that's changed. And football at the highest level, that's even more so. Because the objective is to win. What I think is people will try to disguise that. People try to create what is not true. When people talk about a new generation of coaches... what is that new generation? The generation will always be the ones that win. And the ones that win occasionally or never win will always be something else."

That's not how Van Gaal sees it. "He has more belief in defence than attack," the Manchester United coach told Patrick Barclay for his biography of Mourinho. "My philosophy is always – because I believe we must entertain the public – to have attacking play. His philosophy is to win! That is the difference." And yet there is an element there, surely, of Van Gaal playing to the gallery. Did his AZ Alkmaar side, with its compact 4-4-2, really set out always to attack? Did his Netherlands team at the 2014 World Cup with its counter-attacking 5-3-2? How attacking, really, have United been this season as they've struggled for goals against Aston Villa, Newcastle and Crystal Palace?

"There is no new generation," Mourinho went on. "What there is, is people who've got some idea, some philosophy, and want to create something like, 'We build very well from the back, we have a very good ball possession, we don't play counter-attack...' If you don't play counter-attack then it's because you are stupid. Because counter-attack is a fantastic item of football. It's an ammunition that you have and when you find your opponent unbalanced – because a counter-attack always has a connection with some losing of position because of attacking movements – and when you recover the ball, you have a fantastic moment to score a goal. So if you're not playing counter-attack it's because you're stupid. Because you have to. So I think people are creating – and it has influenced some people in the public opinion. But football will never change in that aspect. Football is to win."

The game against United in April 2015 was a perfect example of that. Chelsea, clear at the top of the table and without Diego Costa, sat deep, played Kurt Zouma alongside Matić at the back of midfield, allowed United to have the ball and, despite having only 30% possession, won 1-0. Although Van Gaal, whose side did play attacking football that day, insisted afterwards that his side had "dominated", the truth was that Chelsea looked comfortable for the vast majority of the game. "It's simple," said Mourinho. "We didn't have important players in our attacking structure. We didn't have Diego Costa. We didn't have the natural replacement for Diego which is [Loïc] Remy. We didn't have depth in our attacking game. We don't have Oscar [he came off the bench], we didn't have a lot of our attacking potential. We needed a point – and our opponent needed three points. It's as simple as that.

"If I don't concede a goal my objective is there. And if my opponent needs to score a goal and their defensive structure, when they lose possession of the ball is very unbalanced – because of the positions they adopt in ball possession, with defenders very exposed, because they project the full-backs a lot and they leave one holding midfield player in front of two central defenders with a big distance in between them... then when you analyse them and you know they do that all the time, if you don't prepare your team for that then you are not coaching.

"Coaching is about recognising the good qualities of the opponents and recognising the fragilities of the opponent. And, more than that, it's to recognise the good qualities of my team – and the bad qualities of my team. Because my team also has bad qualities, and it's very important that me and my players, we recognise our bad qualities. One of the secrets of good coaching is, 'Can you hide your bad qualities from your opponents and even from the pundits?'"

Hiding the bad qualities has become harder this season. This is only the third time Mourinho has reached a third season at any club he's been at. On the previous two occasions – at Chelsea the first time round and at Real Madrid — it's gone horribly wrong.

It was Béla Guttmann, the great Hungarian coach, who noted that "the third season is fatal". Like Mourinho, Guttmann was irascible and brilliant, an itinerant force of nature who fell out with a high proportion of those he worked with. His theory was that after two seasons a coach had said everything he had to say, that the style of play would become predictable, that players would no longer be motivated by the familiar calls to arms, that complacency and decline would inevitably set in. That's the entropic imperative against which all coaches must constantly fight; only a very few – Valeriy Lobanovskyi and Sir Alex Ferguson perhaps most notably – succeed.

There is perhaps a particular issue with Mourinho in that so much of his method relies on his abrasiveness. He conjures conspiracies to forge a siege mentality, he picks fights that often exist nowhere but in his imagination and gradually it wears people down. Journalists and the public roll their eyes as he makes yet another passive aggressive claim that referees are against him, directors tire of his constant hustling and players perhaps weary of his intensity.

That, at least, is the theory. The longer the slump went on, the more significant the uneasiness that had characterised the pre-season tour of the USA came to seem. Mourinho, perhaps, had sensed then that there was something amiss, had felt the lack of hunger, had recognised that certain players had begun to doubt him. By the end of September, it was being widely rumoured that players had been disturbed by Mourinho's attack on certain Sky Sports pundits after they had highlighted misbehaviour by Diego Costa the previous February.

As Chelsea lost to Arsenal in the Community Shield and then picked up just four points from the opening four games of the league season, Mourinho went through his familiar repertoire. He initiated a handshake spat with Arsène Wenger. He publicly berated two members of his medical staff for

treating a player who it turned out was only feigning injury. Eva Carneiro, the team doctor, subsequently left the club and mounted legal proceedings against both Chelsea and Mourinho. Within a few weeks that began to see a terrible miscalculation, not just because of any wrong done to Carneiro personally, but because of her position in the dressing-room. Medical staff, bound as they are by the confidentiality of their profession, often become significant figures in a team's dynamic. They spend time talking to players while treating or examining them and players realise they can trust them. A player may be troubled by, say, a potential problem in his calf that he doesn't want to tell the manger about for fear of being dropped – but he will tell the doctor, who has a duty to investigate and offer advice. A discussion of personal life is often part of the diagnostic process. Issues broached will sometimes be psychological, perhaps especially in sport in which self-confidence is such a major factor. The doctor becomes a trusted outlet. Carneiro, it seems, was popular among the players; ostracising her, it seems, was politically a dreadful move.

For certain players it confirmed a suspicion that, it now appears, had begun to form in early February, when Mourinho attacked Sky for repeatedly showing Diego Costa stamping on Emre Can in the Capital One Cup semi-final, leading to a three-game ban for the striker. Leaks from dressing-rooms have always to be treated with caution but it appears the claims of a conspiracy provoked a sense of embarrassment, that at least some players felt the incident was so obvious that Chelsea should just accept the ban and move on. That is a significant revelation for two reasons:

firstly, because it suggests the failure of Mourinho's familiar circle-the-wagons tactic; and secondly because it has such an obvious parallel in the Torres book, which details player rebelling at being asked to back up Mourinho's claims that the fixture list was biased against Madrid.

As the transfer window drew to a close and it turned out Chelsea's only signings were a reserve goalkeeper, a reserve striker, a reserve centre-back and a promising but unproven left-back, he began to offer veiled criticism of Chelsea's recruitment policy. "You say if you stand still you get worse," he said after the opening draw against Swansea. "It's right." After the defeat to Crystal Palace, the jibes had become more overt. "I gave my club the report of the season projection on April 21," he said, the clear implication being that he had done his job in highlighting targets – John Stones and Paul Pogba most notably – and he could hardly be blamed if others hadn't done theirs. It was very reminiscent of what Mourinho had said in that small room off the tunnel at Adams Park and, to his critics, a classic case of Mourinho promoting his own rather than the club's interests.

And why, it seemed legitimate to ask, had Mourinho had been so keen to sign Radamel Falcao? Perhaps it was just a misjudgment. Perhaps he really did think that, despite the evidence of last season at Manchester United and the Copa América, the Colombian could become again the striker he was before his knee injury. But again a theme of the Torres book seemed relevant, namely the perception among certain Madrid players that Jorge Mendes clients enjoyed a privileged position at the club. Falcao, of course, like Mourinho, is a Mendes client. That is not to imply any wrongdoing, but the closeness of a relationship can lead to misjudgment.

It is one that had had major consequences, largely because of Costa's dismal form. He has gone from being a poacher to a wrestler, the moments of gamesmanship that could once be accepted as a corollary to his edge now the dominant feature about him. He admitted he had returned for pre-season overweight.

Chelsea's preparations for the season in general came under scrutiny. Mourinho, aware of how exhausted his players had looked towards the end of last season, gave them an extra week off in the summer, but far from refreshing them the result seemed to be that they came into the campaign undercooked; that at least offered some explanation for why so many players – Costa, Branislav Ivanović, Cesc Fàbregas, Eden Hazard, Nemanja Matić... – all looked off-form simultaneously. The only player who started the season well was Willian, who had perhaps maintained his levels by playing in the Copa América.

The defensive problems initially caught the eye, with Chelsea's back four against Swansea, Manchester City and West Bromwich Albion undone by simple balls in behind them, exposing John Terry's lack of pace and an unexpected reluctance on the part of Thibaut Courtois to leave his goal-line – perhaps mindful of the goal he conceded to a Charlie Adam shot from the centre-circle against Stoke City last season. But there were problems at the other end as well. Willian's free-kicks for a long time seemed like Chelsea's only mode of attack. After beating Swansea City 5-0 in January, Chelsea scored more than once from open play in a game on just eight of 47 possible occasions.

Chelsea lost at Everton and scrambled a draw at Newcastle. They lost at Porto in the Champions League. They took the lead at home to Southampton but were well-beaten 3-1. Mourinho, having brought on Matić at half-time, took him off again 28 minutes later. Under pressure, the manager counter-attacked. On Sky he spoke uninterrupted for seven minutes: "I want to make it clear... 1) I don't run away; 2) If the club wants to sack me, they have to sack me because I am not running away from my responsibility, my team... 3) Even more important than the second, I think this is a crucial moment in the history of this club. You know why? If the club sacks me, they sack the best manager this club had. And secondly, the message is again the message of bad results. The manager is guilty. This is the message, not just these players, the other ones before, they got [the message] during a decade. This is a moment for everybody to assume their responsibilities. To stick together. This is what I want."

Nobody was quite sure how to take it. The monologue was spectacular, and also included a ludicrous attack on the referee Bobby Madley, who had turned down one good Chelsea shout for a penalty and two for Southampton, and the refereeing establishment in general, as well as a call for everybody at the club to "take responsibility". On the one hand it appeared he was flailing wildly, lashing out at a strong of enemies real and imagined. But the section about his future seemed carefully directed. He

knew he was nearing the edge and was making clear that if he was going he wanted his pay-off. He'd signed a four-year contract in August, but that appears to have a release cause that means he would be due just one year's salary: around £9.5million. But the point about Chelsea's reputation was a sound one. That Mourinho had been re-appointed was itself an indication of how few elite-level managers there are still available to Chelsea. Nobody who dreams of building a dynasty would go there. And yet equally there was the thought, stimulated by the Torres book, of whose line Mourinho was pursuing: was what he said good for him or good for Chelsea?

As results faltered further, others began to wade in. "Mourinho is a great coach but, after a year and a half, he ruins his players," said Fabio Capello. "His players are also psychologically unable to give him what he wants. His cycles tend to last around this period of time."

They beat Aston Villa, but then came a defeat at West Ham in which Matić was sent off just before half-time. Mourinho approached the referee Jon Moss in the tunnel and called him "fucking weak", earing a stadium ban. Was a that a genuine loss of control or was this another example of the trait outlined by Torres of him helping create the appearance of conspiracy to absolve himself of responsibility?

Chelsea went down 3-1 at home to Liverpool. As against Southampton, they'd taken an early lead then dropped deeper and deeper, allowing the away side to gain confidence and momentum. Then, unluckily, with Mourinho banned from the stadium for his attack on Moss, they lost 1-0 at Stoke. It was the first time since Gianluca Vialli was in charge that Chelsea had lost three league games in a row. They'd also gone out of the Capital One Cup to Stoke and struggled to four points in two Champions League games against Dynamo Kyiv. The season has becoming about trying to regain dignity and, if possible, if everything has settled down come the spring, mounting a challenge for fourth or, perhaps, even for the Champions League if the domestic situation means it can be prioritised above all else.

Heading into the international break with a third of the season played, Mourinho still appears to have the confidence of the club, something that can perhaps be explained by three factors. Firstly, there is the terror that he goes elsewhere and enjoys huge success; it may be true that most managerial cycles at the highest level last a decade and it is 12 years since he won the Uefa Cup with Porto, but he has exceeded expectations regularly enough that it seems reasonable to expect further success. Secondly, there are few obvious candidates to step him for him who could realistically be called even a sideways move, never mind an upgrade.

But perhaps most importantly, there is a realisation that Mourinho was probably right to demand greater investment in the summer (albeit with the caveat that he has what must be a frustrating habit of writing off decent players he doesn't warm to – the likes of Kevin De Bruyne, Mohammed Salah, André Schürrle and Juan Cuadrado – and is bafflingly reluctant to give a chance to young players, despite Chelsea enjoying remarkable and sustained success at youth level). This is a squad that has lost a number of leaders recently with the departures of Frank Lampard, Didier Drogba and Petr Cech. John Terry is, finally, showing signs of age. This is a squad that needs carefully nurturing. An interim appointment would find a far trickier situation that those that faced Guus Hiddink, Roberto Di Matteo and Rafa Benítez. Guttman's Three-Year Rule suggests that one of two things must be changed every third season, either the manager or a core of players. Usually, the easier replacement to make is the manager, but here perhaps the reasoning runs that it's better to keep Mourinho and refresh the squad.

That, at least, is a refreshing shift from convention – not just for Chelsea but for modern football as a whole. Whatever went wrong at the start of this season, Mourinho has stayed true to his tactical principles – and that, perhaps, is part of the problem. For those who espouse the Barçajax school, a key principle is continuity; that's why Soriano demanded a willingness to promote academy products when looking for Rijkaard's replacement. It's about a holistic approach – something Soriano is trying to instil at City – and creating a culture at a club (whch in part explains why Manuel Pellegrini was kept on despite last season's disappointment). History tells us that doing that is easier for those whose football is proactive. Reactive coaches, those who deal less in creation than destruction, those who deal not in ideals but in countering those of others, tend to find empire-building far harder. Helenio Herrera, perhaps most notoriously, found his great Internazionale ultimately consumed by its own negativity. When they lost to Celtic in the 1967 European Cup final, it precipitated a collapse that cost them a Serie A title they had seemed sure tow in and ultimately led to Herrera's departure. The full-back Tarcisio Burgnich remembers before that final being corralled in isolation at a hotel in Estoril, the constant focus on stopping Celtic making the squad so stressed that he was woken at night be the sound of nervous teammates vomiting. Mourinho's players may not have reached that pitch of anxiety, but equally his talk when he returned to Stamford Bridge of being the happy one, a leader reading to lay down roots and build an empire, seems further away than ever. But Mourinho remains adamant in his radical reactivity.

A week after the win over United last season, Chelsea held Arsenal at arm's length and drew 0-0 at the Emirates, to which the home fans – with, you hope, some sense of self-irony given their club's own history – chanted "Boring, boring Chelsea". Mourinho responded witheringly. "People talk about style and flair but what is that?" he said. "Sometimes I ask myself about the future, and maybe the future of football is a beautiful green grass carpet without goals, where the team with more ball possession wins the game. The way people analyse style and flair is to take the goals off the pitch."

It's a fine, memorable image – but then the devil always has the best lines. Part of Mourinho's appeal is his cynical charm, which can attract when compared to the prissiness and holier-than-thou attitude of many who promote the Barçajax school. Even Milton seemed to relish Satan's role rather more than those of the denizens of heaven: he was, as William Blake observed, "of the devil's party without knowing it."

But take the pointed hints at Arsenal's impotence away from Mourinho's words, and what emerges is a false dichotomy. Possession does not necessarily equal excitement: there are many who find possession football dull – as demonstrated by the countless complaints about Spain as they won the 2010 World Cup and in 2012 their second European Championship – and there are plenty to thrill to the counter-attacking play of say, Germany at the 2010 World Cup or Borussia Dortmund under Jürgen Klopp.

And this is the irony of Mourinho's position: if, as it often seems, he has allowed his philosophy to be defined in opposition to Barcelona – he is that which they are not – then he is still allowing Barcelona to dictate terms, creating a dichotomy where there could be multiplicity. There is not just radical proactivity and radical reactivity; there are several schools in between.

There are plenty of coaches who have grown up outside the Barçajax school who have been successful, plenty of coaches who have worked out their own way. Given the resources available, Diego Simeone has achieved remarkable success with Atletico, winning La Liga with them and taking them to a Champions League final, and he even plays a game that, like Mourinho's is rooted in struggle, but there is no sense that he consciously sets himself up in contrast to Barça. The greatest influence over him, in fact, still seems to be the great old Argentinian Victorio Spinetto, who coached him in the youth ranks at Vélez Sarsfield and prioritised *fibra* – fibre, or toughness – above all else. There may be doubts about Rafa Benítez's legacy, and it may be that he is beyond the peak of his powers, but he has won a Champions League, two Europa Leagues, two La Liga titles, many of them with teams a little below the highest tier, with a style of play that he honed working in the youth ranks at Real Madrid. His style is different to Mourinho's – and there is a clear antipathy between them – but Benítez just as much as Mourinho likes control; yet he is not defined by Barça. Klopp's star may have fallen a little with his struggles last season, but he developed a devastating form of pressing at Borussia Dortmund that shared certain similarities with the Barçajax approach –

pressuring the man with the ball, pushing high up the pitch – while lacking others – there was none of the Barça focus on maintaining possession.

It is not that there is the Barçajax school and Not-the-Barçajax school; it is that the Barçajax school is one way of playing among an almost infinite variety. As the obsession with Guardiola suggests, Mourinho may have rejected Barcelona as they rejected him, but as the anti-Barcelona he is still defined by them. It may be that the negativity that induces places limitations on how long he can prosper.   Ⓑ

33

Poetry

"More than anyone, you knew what defeat cost."

The Unknown Football Fan

Who even knew you before last Saturday?
True, not many. But you passed away

and they had to deal with you. The tannoy
states you followed the Tigers man and boy
and that last week on the final whistle
your heart lost it's footing and you tippled

from the surge-barrier you'd claimed as yours
onto the terracing at the height of the roar
for the season's first home victory
and surrendered: calm, blue, history.

As the crowd gasped, you were not belittled
to be swept up with the match-day litter,
you were stretchered off like the latest victim
of the opposition's defensive cynicism

with as much right to footballing glory
as those revered for their goal-scoring,
as long and loyal a member
as any businessman on the Board of Directors.

More than anyone, you knew what defeat cost -
beside admission - each game lost
was a bird become extinct: irretrievable,
eternally regrettable,

stirring up a real grief no victory
could remedy. Success was temporary.
Defeat ran and ran. But it was your team.
Your belief was bolstered by being beat.

So consider this your testimonial.
The teams line up like an International
and are presented to your memory.
This minute's silence is your life's trophy
and you could be anyone of us.

The referee convenes the hush.
Footballs lay motionless.
A seagull unfurls above us.
No more walking home in the rain.
No more mid-table clashes away
to South Coast retirement towns or the delirium
of a sixth-round Cup run.

Your wife won't be expecting you. Your tea
won't be ready and your scarf splits it's seams
behind the kitchen door, all accepting the fact
that your game's over when the dirt's smoothed flat.

Yet we stand and feel the chill you felt
Blowing up from the Boothferry Road end
and the emptiness that mocks us
like the space cleared for the executive boxes

and we miss you, Unknown Football Fan,
though we missed your name in the clatter to stand.
You were never mentioned in the Green Papers
but you fell among fellow believers.

We know the referee will restart the game.
Our blood will glide like a ball in rain.
We will root and sing. We will feel aggrieved
until our own irretrievable defeat.

We hold death only in abeyance.
So in your physical absence,
in the spirit of thinking of you
we know the sporting thing to do
is to lift your trophy and kiss it
for the full triumph of your final minute.

Craig Smith

A Striker Fires Wide

With the lid of the cup as a cap.
On my teammates' shoulders
like an open-topped carriage,
with both camps singing
linking banners like bunting
and with the stadium like a station
announcing my arrival
to a civic reception
of the tea-time viewing public:
yes, I would have ridden that train.

Glory. Pushed wide
by the laces of my boots.
four cool steps and then nothing,
the ball, its logo, its trademark and stitching
trundling off into the goalmouth's sidings,
past the post and past the netting
past a terrace of photographers
exquisitely recording
the ball at rest
beside the buffer of the hoardings.
And the crowd. Punctured
by the final whistle.

I've forgotten what I was going to say.
Ah, yes: the boy can do
what the man cannot.
Something like that.
Even if and when the ball runs true
then to lift my kicking foot,
to swing, to follow through
is to risk ridicule.
What if the turf breaks up
with a longer stud.
What if a defender passes through
my standing foot.
What if written through the way
my weight redistributes.

I was worth my weight in newsprint,
the glowing tribute to a golden generation.
I would leap, sure
the earth would rise to meet me
and land me safely, securely,
They called up the wildest hyperbole
of shipping and aviation
and astro-navigation
to explain my movements
and their fascination.
My shirt was a sail strung
on the rigging of my chest.
I used the gravity of each victory
to sling me toward my next trajectory,
my next trophy.
I was a tax on poor defending.
Salesmen studied my feint and dummy.
I would switch across a speeding ball
like a circus horseman
impressing his girl.
Loops, radii, parabola, pi:
my through ball was geometry.
I expressed myself trigonometrically.
The ball stood accused.
I was the one to answer to.
Now the ground does not run true.

Stones rip my knees apart.
The earth refuses to cushion my fall.
Even my hair follows its own course.
It affects me.
It pulls my shirt chasing long balls
and bobbles the ball as I shoot.
I'm left a yard short
susceptible to injury gasping for breath
on the touchline with a dead-leg
as they bring me off again.

Each night I defeat myself.
The penalty. Relived, re-run, retaken.
From the dug-out.
From the terrace. The concession's stand.
The director's box.
From the TV station with the rights
to the footage long since bought.
From the vantage point of my own head.
I send the keeper the wrong way
and still it comes to naught.
I imagine a man in the highest stand, laughing.
I see a kid with his father, distraught.

Children: be selfish.
Be greedy. Takes chances.
Do the unexpected.
Give the keeper the eyes
and force him to get dirty.
Perform the dance you choreographed
in the nation's living room
with the corner flag as your partner
and cheering as your tune.
Know you're worth it.
Fill your boots.

But do not know yourself.
It's no use.

Craig Smith

39

Memories

"The best player on the pitch was a boyish little inside-left with glowing blond hair."

The Immortality of Awfulness

In 1965-66, Tasmania Berlin played their only Bundesliga season becoming the worst team in history

By Felix Lill and Javier Sauras

Berlin is notorious for footballing underachievement: neither of the only two professional clubs, Hertha BSC from the former West and Union from the East, has ever represented the German capital in an adequate way. But 50 years ago, at the hottest point of the Cold War, things looked even worse. The underdogs Tasmania 1900 suddenly had to stand for Berlin in the Bundesliga — and they set every conceivable record for being terrible.

Football isn't what it used to be? Back in the day, people claim, everything was more fun. The crowds still came to see footballers rather than social media superstars. The playing standards may not have been comparable with today but at least there were characters on the pitch: many were brutal destroyers, but the elegant few raised the spirits. After the game, some of these tough men would light a fag, down a beer or give an interview with crude vocabulary. There was something more real about those figures compared with today's immaculate athletes with their good looks and carefully anodyne post-match statements. The grounds were different, too: again, not as good, comfortable and safe as today. But they felt like a real home, rather than a sterile multi-event complex. That's the theory.

There is probably no place in the world where these prejudices are as obviously both true and false as in the Werner-Seelenbinder-Sportpark in Neukölln, a working-class district in Germany's capital that has undergone significant gentrification. On a sunny Sunday afternoon, the stands are half empty and an echo lingers in the air after the coach shouts at his players. Those dressed in white and blue, the favourites, score a quick but deserved goal with a header. True: back in the day, this club would rarely be considered favourites, let alone manage to be on a winning run, even if it was on home soil as today.

"Tasmaa-nia, Tasmaa-nia!" As Hagen Nickelé, coordinator of the ultra supporters, chants the first line with the rhythm of the Italian national anthem, the handful of others know their response: "TASMAA-NIA, FAN-TAS-TI-CA!" On his day off, all seems good to Hagen Nickelé. His beloved Tasmania 1973 Berlin dominate the game and they might close the season among the top three in the Berlin-Liga, the capital's top division — part of the sixth tier nationally. "We wanted to be promoted this year," explains Nickelé, a blond-haired fan from northern Germany dressed in the white-and-blue of his side, "but it's not that easy, you know." Other teams have invested notable sums in their squads.

Even in division six, competition is tough these days. "But of course," Nickelé adds without being asked, "this is not comparable to the financial situation back then." Although Tasmania never were a rich club, they used to list full-time professionals on their payroll. Today, players are happy to get some pocket money, free beer and sausages after home games.

In many ways, downsized Tasmania Berlin have been, and still are, going against the trend. "We like the underdog image," says another ultra in the stands, Ulrich Timm. Born in 1950, 18 years before Nickelé, his supporters club's boss, Timm has experienced all eras of the club. As a child, he was raised during the great times of the late 1950s. In his adolescence, Timm learned what it meant to root for a team that had become a national joke. And because he was faithful enough to suffer more, he experienced the bitter years of sporting over-ambition and financial demise as a young adult. Later, Timm supported the renaissance of the love of his youth. "Tasmania," this retiree dressed in an old jersey explains, "is all this suffering taken together. You can't come here without knowing our history."

"Kevin! Get up and don't complain!" A shout flies over the stands and extends to the other fields beyond. The coach's voice is so loud that it hurts – though partly because the bench is only five metres from away most of the spectators. Even Ulrich Timm, whose ears no longer serve him as they once did, soon stops waving his decades-old handmade white-and-blue flag. Tasmania are already 2-0 ahead: things are going absolutely as planned. But

the coach's temper is challenged by his striker, Kevin Lenz, who fell to the ground after a soft tackle. "You're not playing for Hertha, you understand?!"

The tall forward Kevin Lenz is not nearly agile enough to play in the Bundesliga, nor does he have the technique or stamina. But here in Neukölln, the historical underdogs draw some of their pride from their opposition to Berlin's big club, the Bundesliga side Hertha BSC. Clearly, it's a one-sided rivalry: while many of the Hertha players signed from foreign clubs may not even have heard about this mediocre amateur club, all Tasmanians unite behind one cause. Nickelé puts it into a simple statement: "We all feel a very strong aversion to Hertha BSC."

Is it envy? Hertha play in Berlin's biggest sporting venue, the Olympic Stadium, which today holds 76,000 spectators. Through the trashy-sounding loudspeakers of Tasmania's Werner-Seelenbinder-Sportpark, an old man's voice announces today's match attendance: "We thank 80 visitors for coming!" Next to the pitch, a handful of boys dressed in Tasmania track suits are playing and their ball sometimes flies onto the field of the adults. There is little commitment to ameliorate the irritation: were these boys asked for which club they'd rather play, the answer would almost certainly be Hertha, not Tasmania.

"We're a club in opposition," insists Nickelé. It is as much a description of himself as of his favourite club. Nickelé, 47 years old, moved to Berlin 20 years ago. "I did not like the commercialism of most clubs," he says. "In Berlin, Hertha BSC were very much like that." The alternative would have been FC Union Berlin, located in East Berlin and today playing in the Second Bundesliga. But East German history and the club's nostalgia about it did not seem an option.

For lovers of football history like Nickelé, there was another choice: Tasmania 1973 Berlin. "People who have been following German football more seriously know this club." To be sure, there is this stigma of being the worst ever. But isn't this also what makes Tasmania unlike all other clubs? Especially in Berlin, Tasmania 1973 Berlin may even be the obvious choice for a football lover with sceptical feelings towards today's levels of commercialisation.

The capital city of Europe's most populous and economically powerful country has always tried to be a football hub. But for one reason or another it mostly failed. After the Second World War, when football became more widely popular, clubs in West Berlin lagged behind those from other areas. The East Berlin powerhouse BFC Dynamo Berlin, sponsored by the socialist government's secret police, the Stasi, won nine consecutive East German championships. But when Germany reunified in 1990, the club was politically stigmatised. It has been an amateur club for many years now. In the Bundesliga, the financially well-equipped Hertha have a history of bad management. In the 1980s and 1990s, the club mostly played in the second division. For more than a decade, Germany's top flight was played without a club from the capital.

But because rich Hertha have often disappointed, there has been room for challengers from the city. Once, 50 years ago, the chance of the Tasmanians had come. "That year in the Bundesliga probably killed us," moans Ulrich Timm. But, he adds, "it also made us immortal." There has never been a worse Bundesliga team than Tasmania in 1965-66.

How did this happen? "Actually, we should have played in the Bundesliga from its first season," remembers Hanns Leske, a 65-year-old companion of Timm who earned a PhD in sports history and wrote a widely acclaimed book about his club entitled *Der ewige Letzte* (*Always the Last*). In that historic season for Tasmania, Leske was 15 years old. A passionate supporter of the club, he wrote down all line-ups in a notebook, travelled to away games and gathered a private collection of documents about Tasmania. When Leske talks about his club, though, he cannot avoid mentioning Hertha. This is not just because Tasmanians consider Hertha arrogant: they also think their place in the Bundesliga unfair. "I mean," Leske says in an almost apologetic tone like someone who is reluctantly repeating his core message over and over again, "I have proven in my book that they sneaked their way into the Bundesliga. They should not have played there from the beginning."

What Leske means is this: until 1963, West German football was structured on a regional basis, with regional champions who would then compete in a play-off system for the national championship. For the 1963-64 season this system was changed to a national league– the Bundesliga. In the run-up, most expected that those clubs who had been most successful over the previous three or four years would play in the first edition of the Bundesliga. Had that happened,

Tasmania would have secured their spot in the Bundesliga: the side had recently won three consecutive Berlin titles and in 1962 even came third in all West Germany. But before the end of the 1963 season, the president of Hertha, who had good connections with the political and regulatory authorities, received a confidential message from the Deutscher Fußballbund (DFB), Germany's national football federation: to qualify for the first Bundesliga season, the single spot for Berlin was going to the team that won the 1963 regional championship.

"Tasmania's president had no idea about this arbitrary rule. Everybody thought the successes in previous years would suffice, so the management had not invested in the team in 1963," says Leske. That year, Hertha took the Berlin title and thus secured the significant Bundesliga revenues coming from gate receipts, media coverage and other sources. The West German capital's footballing hierarchy was clear: Hertha were the number one. But not for long. After two sobering seasons, finishing 14th out of 16 teams both times, Hertha tried to improve by spending big. But Hertha's managers paid bigger salaries and cash bonuses than were allowed. As a result, the club that many thought should not have been part of the Bundesliga in the first place were relegated.

This was not just a sports scandal. In 1965, the citizens of Berlin citizens were very aware of their position on the front line of the Cold War. Three years earlier, the Cuban missile crisis had almost precipitated another world war. Berlin was in its fourth year as a divided city, characterised by the high wall erected by the East German government. Although

West Berlin belonged to the "free world", its locked-in citizens struggled to leave their territory. In response to this crisis, the hometown of Hertha and Tasmania became a capitalist enclave pampered by the Western partners: citizens of West Berlin were exempt from the otherwise mandatory military service and the city received subsidies from the other West German federal states. The West wanted to demonstrate the supremacy of liberal democracy over socialism.

"Having a Bundesliga season without a team from Berlin was just unthinkable," recalls Leske. Of the many levels on which the two Germanies fought a battle about who was more successful, sport was one of the most important because of its public visibility. Football was arguably the most popular sport on both sides of the border. With Tasmania seething after being overlooked for the Bundesliga's opening season, DFB officials had little choice but to offer them the vacant spot. In a sense, it was a belated victory over their local rivals and all the others the Tasmanians felt had betrayed them.

But Tasmania's management were told of their promotion only two weeks before the start of the 1965-66 season. Nobody was prepared. Deutschlandfunk and Radio Luxemburg broadcast messages for the Tasmania players who were on holiday in various parts of Europe, calling on them to come home soon to get ready for the Bundesliga adventure. "Tasmania players," the message said, "please report yourselves immediately." The defender Helmut Fiebach, for example, was found by local policemen on a camp site in Austria, while others were lying on the beaches of Spain or Italy.

"That message reached me on the Baltic coast," recalls Hans-Günter Becker, the team's captain. "Of course, I packed my bags immediately." So did others. And although it was difficult to land big signings to improve a squad that had been expected to play in the second tier, the club's managers did pick up Horst Szymaniak, who had been a star of the Italian club Varese. Szymaniak was 30 and already beyond his peak, but thanks to his experience with the West Germany national side he was to become the team's leader. With him in the squad, there was at least hope that Tasmania could represent Berlin in a respectable way.

"But to be honest," Becker says, "we knew from the beginning that we had no chance." Which was not to say that anyone was hesitant to give it a try. "We all wanted to embark on this adventure although from the beginning, I told everybody that it may be smarter to write a letter to the football association, saying something like, 'Dear DFB, thank you very much for considering us, but we'd better keep training for another year.'" That letter was never written. Instead, the players, until that point mostly amateurs, were asked to scale back their regular jobs, become full-time professionals and start the season with almost no preparation. Becker, an employee with a local public authority, was lucky to have an understanding superior. "I told him: 'Hey boss, from now I can only work part-time. But don't worry, it'll only last eight months.'" The boss agreed and a year later praised his employee: "Great to have you back as before, Becker. I knew I could count on you!"

At first, the players could also count on their hometown. The Berlin newspaper BZ ran a front-page headline "We need a chant for our new Bundesliga side" and suggested the rhyme "Ra-ra-ra, Tas-ma-nia". Even East Berlin's papers were taking an interest in the class enemy's side. Hardly surprisingly, the mood at the first game of the season was euphoric. In a packed Olympic Stadium, where so far Hertha had been playing their games, more than 80,000 came to see the underdogs. The visitors Karlsruhe, a nominally stronger team with a history among the elite, were the obvious favourites. But the impossible happened: the Tasmania forward Wulf-Ingo Usbeck, nicknamed 'Ringo' because of his resemblance to the Beatles drummer, scored a first goal, followed by another. Karlsruhe were too shocked to get their act together. Tasmania won their first match in a stadium where they didn't belong, in a league where they didn't belong.

Within two weeks, though, Tasmania were back as underdogs. They slipped into a relegation spot and defeat followed upon defeat. No wonder: many of the players kept their jobs in the form of part-time arrangements. Only one training session per day was possible and the team's fitness level lagged behind that of the competition. And the few players who had no job on the side would kill their free mornings with alcohol. Of the star player Horst Szymaniak, it was said that he regularly came fully drunk to the evening training sessions, next to a baker who had started work at 5.30am or railway officials who would sometimes arrive late because of the workload during the daily rush hour. "The Tasmania side was an unequal team in many ways, and even a drunken Szymaniak was still the best footballer," says Leske.

As the season went on, the early euphoria faded away in most aspects. The Olympic Stadium changed face, from the proud and threatening sporting temple it had been designed as into some sort of abandoned battlefield: there wasn't much doubt who would lose the games once Tasmania came onto the pitch nor did many fans come to witness the spectacles. Whether in the East or West, Germans were split between laughing about the Tasmanians and feeling sorry. A popular joke of the time asked when Tasmania has last won a game, and the response was: "ask your grandfather". When the season's first half came to a close, Tasmania was already so far behind that relegation had almost become an arithmetic certainty.

"As the season went on," recalls the striker Jürgen Wähling, "being one of the eleven on the pitch turned into a sort of punishment." German football regulations did not at that point allow substitutions, increasing the suffering, especially for defenders and the goalkeeper. "Sooner or later, I lost the enjoyment of playing football," said the goalkeeper Hans-Joachim Posinski, nicknamed 'Jockel'. Some fans may have contributed to this feeling. When the other goalkeeper, Heinz Rohloff, on 30 April 1966 let in a third against Eintracht Frankfurt, parts of the Tasmania crowd lay down a wreath. Behind the flowers, a large banner showed the number 100 – the team had just conceded a century of Bundesliga goals.

The 1965-66 season marked a year of Bundesliga records, most of which were established by the Tasmanians and have not been broken. Most prominently, there is the points tally of eight out of

sixty-eight – the worst performance of all time. The goal difference was the worst as well: no other team has since scored as few as 15 goals in a season and none ever conceded as many as Tasmania's 108. Also, no other team won fewer games in an entire season than Tasmania with two in total and none away. The 28 defeats are another historical best, or worst. Neither has any side suffered 10 losses in a row or gone 31 consecutive matches without a victory. Also, no team so far has attracted as few as 827 spectators in one game, as Tasmania did in their winter encounter at home against Borussia Mönchengladbach. Of the all-time Bundesliga table, summing up all seasons so far and thus currently ranking 53 teams, every German with a solid interest in football knows the occupants of two spots: the first are record champions Bayern Munich, the last are Tasmania 1900 Berlin.

After the one-year adventure, relegation didn't just mean a step back to normality. A credit of 150,000 Deutsche Mark from the football association and the sale of the most prominent players – Horst Szymaniak joined the Swiss side FC Biel and the 22-year-old forward Wulf-Ingo Usbeck moved to Nürnberg – helped avoid immediate financial collapse. But for a club that still enjoyed no privileged connections with either the political or economic elites risking expenditures that exceeded revenues proved unsustainable. "Tasmania had always been a club of simple people and was financially quite limited," says Leske. As a result, in 1973, after various attempts to achieve promotion to the top-flight again, the holders of all negative Bundesliga records were overwhelmed by a debt burden of 800,000 Deutsche Mark. Tasmania 1900 Berlin filed for bankruptcy and were consigned to history.

Leske, then in his early twenties, belonged to those who helped establish a successor. In the year 1900, drinking seafarers and workers had been sitting in a public house in Berlin and founded, from of a feeling of melancholia and wanderlust, a sports club to be named after a far-away Australian island. The logo was to include the dog-like animal from there – the Tasmanian devil. In 1973, the newly founded SV Tasmania Neukölln, starting anew from the lowest and most provincial division, took over as many relics of the failed predecessor as possible, including the image of the devil. Hanns Leske, who later became part of the club's board, steered attempts to reach the playing level of earlier days. But as money was lacking and the road through the lower leagues proved rockier than expected, the Tasmanians got stuck on the way.

In the 1990s, a real estate investor pumped money into the club and temporarily lifted Tasmania to sixth place in the Oberliga, the fourth division. The crushing defeats from the Bundesliga year had made the club sufficiently prominent to attract new donors, though all such engagements would turn out to be short-lived. Once the first sugar daddy departed, Tasmania went into free-fall through the amateur divisions, until an apartment building firm showed interest and in 2000 also bought the license to appear in the club's name – turning it into Tasmania Gropiusstadt. Under the brief reign of the company, the club reached the fifth tier, but soon slid again. Since 2012, without the backing of a rich

institution or individual, the team today called SV Tasmania Berlin have been playing in the sixth division. "We have the potential to reach the fifth at least," insists Nickelé as he rolls up his Tasmania flag after the victory in the Werner-Seelenbinder-Sportpark. "We want to be the club of this part of town and establish an authentic image."

A football lover throughout his life, Nickelé was born in Hanover and later lived in Hamburg for many years. "My hometown club Hannover 96 has been practically bought up by a local businessman who cares more about money than football. And the big team in Hamburg, HSV, are a rich club without soul or even success." In discussions between the Tasmania board and the ultras, Nickelé uses these two as shocking examples for what a club can lose when financial matters leave of popular control. "We want to be more like Hamburg's second club, FC St. Pauli." World-renowned and popular, St Pauli play in Germany's second division and have for years been marketing themselves as an alternative, punk-rock and left-wing club, though it has long become a successful business venture. "Sure, there are compromises," says Nickelé, "if you want to improve."

How far does the club want to improve, and would another sugar daddy with deeper pockets be acceptable to achieve such goals? Hanns Leske doesn't care much anymore. "I parted from the club a while ago," he says in a sober voice on the telephone. "I didn't like the attempts with instant money." Why does he not even come to his old club's traditional stadium anymore to see some games, why does he not care how the

Tasmanians are doing today? Leske cannot give a clear answer, rather an apparent mixture of anecdotes and moral rules, typical of an emotionally attached man: "You know, it's no longer what it used to be. After all that has happened to the club, these newer constellations called Tasmania have too little in common with the original. Tasmania 1900 was the love of my youth." One that may not have been an easy love, but it was unforgettable.

The Stench of the White Elephants

Only now is the full scale of the corruption that surrounded the Brazil World Cup beginning to emerge.

By Jamil Chade

A few days after the final of the World Cup, the most expensive stadium in Brazil and third-most expensive in the world staged another event: 100 couples held their wedding party at the ground that had served as one of the main venues for the World Cup. The event was broadcast by TV Globo, which paid for part of the World Cup rights and largely blocked any criticism of the event. In the TV report, the company insisted that the mass wedding had been a source of "great emotion" and that the stadium had created new opportunities.

With only two teams – Brasiliense and Luziânia, both of which play in the fourth division of Brazilian football — the Federal District became the image of the World Cup scandal and its non-existent legacy. Months after the World Cup final, the lack of games at the stadium obliged the government to transfer part of its bureaucracy to the Mané Garrincha, using the rooms for various different departments. The outside was turned into garage for city buses. A year after the World Cup, the deficit of the stadium was more than R$3.5 million (£610,000).

The reality is that the costumes have been taken off, Fifa has folded up the circus tent and is now preparing for its next venture: in Russia in 2018. A sports depression took over Brazil after the national championship with its absent public and their missing star players returned to occupy the millionaire arenas used at the World Cup. The illusion created by the World Cup was over.

Fifa may have enjoyed record income from the event, but the situation of Brazilian stadiums is radically different. Eight of the twelve arenas completed the first year after the World Cup with losses totalling R$120 million. Worse, there are no prospects of recovering the money invested.

In Manaus, the Amazonian teams have avoided using the World Cup stadium for the state championship games. The Arena, which cost R$2.5bn to build, costs R$700,000 per month in maintenance. But between the end of the World Cup and February 2015, the stadium hosted only seven games. Losses exceeded R$2.7m in one year. On average, the attendance at the 2015 Amazonas football championship was 659 people per game.

In Natal, the ABC club broke an agreement with the consortium that manages the Arena das Dunas. A contract provided that derbies were held in the stadium but in early March the match between ABC and America was held at another location, the Frasqueirao. America kept their games at the Arena, but in seven matches, the average gate was only 3500 – 10% of stadium capacity.

Even the Maracanã struggles to contain the financial deficit. To generate a profit for administrators, the stadium needs at least 30,000 fans per game. In the state championship in 2015, the average attendance was no more than 3600 per game. In the case of Flamengo, the average is 16,000. Result: a loss of R$77m in the first year after the World Cup. In January 2015, the Pantanal Arena in Cuiabá was forced to close its doors for "urgent" rennovations.

The World Cup was followed by a series of allegations and investigations into the costs of works and contracts. One year after the final, federal police launched Operation Fair Play, ironically using Fifa's slogan. In August 2015, the authorities announced an investigation into claims that the Odebrecht construction company had won the tender for the construction of the Arena Pernambuco thanks to fraud and had overpriced the work by R$42.8m. The suspicion was that public officials were bribed to favour the construction.

Despite high costs, Recife ended up with only five World Cup matches, including four during the first phase. "We have indications that there was overpricing," confirmed the Federal Police Chief Marcello Diniz Cordeiro. In June 2015, the president of the construction company, Marcelo Odebrecht, was arrested, accused of involvement in bribery in various projects.

Initially, the bidding was opened by the government of Eduardo Campos, who was killed in a plane crash in August 2014. The expected expenditure was R$532m. But when construction was over, the final cost was R$700m. The contract also stipulated that the state government would pay back Odebrecht for 30 years for possible revenue shortfalls at the stadium site and in projects taking place on neighbouring land.

The contract not only granted the right to build the Arena, but also to exploit commercially an area of Recife. According to a study by the Court of Pernambuco, this commitment meant that the state would transfer to the construction company a total of R$1.8bn over three decades. The suspicion is that Odebrecht allied itself to government officials in order to secure the financing facilities to build the stadium.

What the Federal Police also found was that the Organising Committee responsible for the construction of the Arena Pernambuco was led by the person who was elected, three years later, as the mayor of Recife, Geraldo Julio. The same Committee also included Paulo Camara, who later became state governor. In 2009, when the contract of the stadium was being negotiated, they were respectively President and Vice President of the Steering Committee of the Arena.

But the allegations of corruption are not only found in Recife. In August 2015, police seized spreadsheets and data in several Odebrecht offices in Brazil

It's suspected that the works at the Pernambuco Arena were not the only ones to involve overpricing.

Also in August 2015, a report from the Bahia Court of Auditors revealed overpricing in the works of the Arena Fonte Nova. In 2010, the stadium was built thanks to a contract between the state government and a consortium that included Odebrecht and OAS. The Court concluded that, in the public-private partnership agreement, the amount transferred from the government of Bahia to the companies would come to R$107m a year by 2025, an amount of money considered "excessive". The report was delivered to the Federal Police, which began to investigate the case.

OAS, the company that administers the stadium, had their shares blocked by the courts as a result of the anti-corruption operations in Brazil, known as Lava Jato, the biggest investigation into corruption in the history of the country, and may be forced to sell their assets in the arena.

The corruption scandal also touched the works of Arena Corinthians, built by Odebrecht in Itaquera, in an area where there happened to be Petrobras pipelines. The pipes were removed in February 2012, but when the police studied the spreadsheets of accounts operated by Alberto Youseff, a known criminal who has been convicted of black-market financial dealings, they found the name of the stadium and work on the pipes. In the end, the stadium's cost reached R$1.3bn, more than 42% higher than originally planned by the organisers.

The German engineering company Bilfinger confirmed in March 2015 that it had identified "possible improper payments" for contracts at the World Cup. "In the course of internal investigations into potential violations, Bilfinger has reviewed the activities of the group's companies in Brazil for several months," said a company statement. "After reviewing all transactions in recent years, reports indicate that a potential improper payment exists of US$1m in total."

The suspicion is that Brazilian officials of a government agency collected bribes to offer contracts to the company. In 2014 the company signed contracts with the Brazilian government valued at a total of R$21.2m. In addition to the World Cup, the company provides services to Petrobras, the National Petroleum Agency, the Federal Senate and Anatel, the National Telecommunications Agency. There were R$13m in contracts just for the supply of 1500 monitors and software for the Centre for Integrated Command and Control for the tournament. The system was considered one of the main legacies of the World Cup and led to the centralisation of the security operation.

According to the German company, they were audited by Ernst & Young and Deloitte. "Bilfinger received inside information last year indicating that there may have been violations of ethical regulations by the group about providing monitors for the security centres in major Brazilian cities," explained the company in a statement. "The company just opened a full investigation into the case. The complaint is linked to suspected bribery by Bilfinger employees in Brazil to civil servants and state officials."

For anyone who was in the heart of the World Cup organisation, the case of Bilfinger sounds like just the tip of the iceberg of a system fitted to ensure profits not only for builders and for Fifa but also for accomplices, governments, civil servants and tens of intermediaries, even if it has meant wasting billions of Reais and a non-existent legacy. Brazil has undoubtedly been looted. And Fifa knew it.

When I asked Sepp Blatter at the last day of the World Cup what he thought would be done with the Brazilian stadiums, he replied by drawing a question mark in the air. When, a year after the World Cup, I asked a high-ranking official at Fifa what they thought of empty stadiums and the debt in the accounts, he just smiled and said, "It is no longer our problem."

This is an edited extract from Jamil Chade's new book, Política, Propina e Futebol, *published by Objetiva.*

For the Love of the Honest Men

An Ayr United fan reflects on decades of following the ups and downs at Somerset Park

By Ally Palmer

There's a framed signed football shirt hanging on my office wall. It's a rather fetching black Adidas top, sponsored by an online betting firm. It's signed by what turned out to be one of the least successful squads in the history of Ayr United Football Club, but it's a treasured memento from one of my favourite seasons. To understand why, I need to go back a few decades.

I've been following Ayr United since I was five. I say 'following' because officially not all that time has been spent 'supporting' them. And I've subjected my two children to the same thing since they were old enough to notice, despite being brought up in Edinburgh, which is about 80 miles from Ayr.

My first game was as a five year old. I think the opposition was East Fife. They certainly wore gold and black stripes, or so it seemed from the back of the cowshed. But it was foggy and my memory is foggier still. Whoever the opposition, I had officially been introduced to football.

Despite growing up in Tollcross, Glasgow, within a brisk walk of Celtic Park, my dad had supported Rangers all his life. He didn't drive so Saturday visits to Ibrox were out of the question. Instead we became regular visitors to our nearest football ground, Somerset Park in Ayr.

Somehow in the mind of a boy, the local team is never enough, and peer pressure soon meant that I had to make a choice. It was the choice faced by most young boys growing up in the west of Scotland: Rangers or Celtic? Because of my dad, I chose Rangers. To make matters worse, the Rangers I chose were not the nine-in-a-row vintage. My Rangers didn't win all that much apart from the small matter of a European Cup-Winners Cup.

But somehow, I managed to square my misplaced allegiance to Rangers with my weekly visits to Somerset Park.

I can see now that there was something special about watching Ayr United, or even Ayr United reserves, but at the time it was just something I did. On occasional Saturdays, when I visited my grandparents, I would be taken to Celtic Park to watch the side that would become the Lisbon Lions. We even attended the 1967 Scottish Cup final between Celtic and Aberdeen where the crowd was an incredible 126,102. In the mind of a young football fan, we were definitely the 'two'.

By the time I faced up to the truth that I wasn't actually a Rangers fan, I had been to Celtic Park many times and Ibrox only once. Not surprisingly, the opposition that day was Ayr United.

There was, for a while, a personal connection. My brother-in-law played for Ayr. I was ten when my sister came home one night and casually mentioned she was working with an Ayr United player. It took a while to sink in. She knew a real, living and breathing, part-time footballer. Previously I hadn't imagined that footballers, even Ayr players, had everyday lives. That night I looked out a recent programme and she pointed him out. The picture on the front couldn't have been more than five inches wide with twenty-odd players in the line-up, but I was able to give a full description. I was able to tell her his name, Billy Walker; his position, left midfield; and how good he was, classic left-half, slight of build, great passer of the ball and with bandy legs that John Wayne would have been proud of.

Not long after that he came round to the house in his white Mini with the miniature Adidas football boots hanging from the mirror. It was one of the most thrilling nights of my young life and I took to him immediately. He was the big brother I never had. He soon became part of the family. So much so that on the night that Neil Armstrong became the first man to walk on the moon he sat up with my mum to watch it. She told me she would wake me up when it happened but she never did. I would remind her of this for many years to come.

My conversion to being an official Ayr United supporter was a long process. I see now that Ayr had been nagging away at my loyalties for years. This was a time when Ayr were as often in the old First Division as the Second. They were in the original Premier Division and stayed there for the first three seasons. I can still clearly remember the evening when a win against Motherwell secured their place in the newly formed league. There were tears in my eyes. There would be many more to come.

This was a time of Ally MacLeod, Dixie Ingram, Quentin 'Cutty' Young and Johnny Doyle. Ayr regularly beat the Old Firm and reached cup semi-finals. Unfortunately they never managed to do both at the same time.

I travelled to Hampden one wet Wednesday night in 1973 as the only Rangers supporter on the Prestwick Cricket Club bus. My dad was a non-playing member who enjoyed the cheap beer as much as the cricket. I remember the scarf I wore was made of blue silk. It was a Scottish Cup semi-final and Rangers won 2-0. Three seasons earlier Ayr had taken Celtic to a replay in the League Cup semi-final. Ayr were winning 3-2 with minutes to go, then Celtic equalised. I was there on 8 October 1969 for the replay. It was a day after my twelfth birthday so I presume it was a late present. Ayr lost 2-1. The great Celtic goalkeeper Ronnie Simpson was carried off with a dislocated shoulder and I cried. Again.

If Ayr had won that game, they would have played St Johnstone in the final and Europe would have been but a victory away. Instead, Ayr played Clyde at Shawfield on the same day. Agonisingly, going to Clyde's ground involved driving past Hampden Park.

So what made me face up to the reality and ditch Rangers for good?

On reflection the answer is easy. On 11 October 1975 Ayr played Rangers at Somerset Park. Three days earlier I had celebrated my eighteenth birthday. I stood in the enclosure with a Celtic-supporting friend. He was shouting for Ayr while I did my best for Rangers. The final score was 3-0 to Ayr. My heart wasn't in it. Rangers won the treble that year and I felt nothing. At last, some of the confusions of adolescence had begun to resolve themselves. I was an Ayr United supporter and I was finally proud to admit it.

Was it worth it? In some ways from a purely footballing sense the answer was yes. Despite being a part-time club we were competing with teams that were winning European trophies. We were playing exciting football. We had a reserve team who won the First Division with crowds of many thousands. I know as I was there most weeks; in those days the reserve fixture list was the same as the first team's.

I was at Somerset Park on 13 September 1969 when a crowd of 25,225 somehow squeezed into the ground for the visit of Rangers. Squeezed in so much in fact that fans spilled over the wall and had to be accommodated on the 'running track'.

Players were going on to greater things. Dick Malone to the Cup-winning Sunderland team, Davie Stewart to Leeds United where he played in a European Cup final, Cutty Young to Coventry and then Rangers (I followed Coventry for a few years because of him) and Dixie Ingram to Nottingham Forrest. Johnny Doyle became the first Ayr player in more than 40 years to win a full cap. We were in the first Premier League. But three years later we were relegated and it's been a gradual decline ever since.

There have been periods of hope. The early 80s saw another League Cup semi-final appearance against Dundee with Stevie Nicol and Robert Conner forming a hugely talented full-back pairing that threatened to replace Danny McGrain and Sandy Jardine in the Scotland team.

This was also a period of clever dealings in the transfer market. In 1979, Joe Fillipi, our honest but raw fullback went to Celtic in return for Brian McLaughlin and £100,000. He turned out to be one of the greatest ever players to wear the black and white. A few weeks after he signed, he scored the winner in a league game against Celtic. The writing was on the wall for the great Jock Stein.

Then there was Ally MacLeod: the main reason I spell my name the way I do. He was in charge during the vintage period of the late 60s and early 70s where he instilled a belief in his teams that they could beat anyone. He was manager during the time when my brother-in-law played for Ayr and he still won't hear a bad word said about Ally. We rescued him from the pain of Argentina and he took us to the Second Division championship in 1988. That team had, in John Sludden, a genuinely deadly striker with zero pace and Henry Templeton, who was given the MacLeod kiss-of-death when Ally hailed him as Scotland's answer to Peter Beardsley. Henry was in that great Scottish tradition, the diminutive winger. He was known by some as 'Kneecaps', due to the lack of any bare thigh between his shorts and his socks. And this was a time when shorts were short. He was a joy to watch.

That season of record goals, points and wins was crowned when we beat Alloa to ensure promotion. A pitch invasion ensued. It was a precious moment of euphoria and I found myself with the rest of the crowd, running impulsively across the turf. I managed to track down Sludden and get his signature. "There you go, son," the youthful Sludden said. He was 23. I was 32. But I was very happy.

This was also the period in the club's history that most Scottish football supporters remind you of when you mention you are an Ayr United fan. We had our 'what if' moment. A Scottish businessman who grew up supporting Ayr offered to buy the club, claiming he would have the then Second Division champions playing in Europe within five years. The shareholders rejected the bid probably because Ally MacLeod threatened to resign if it was successful. His name was David Murray. He soon bought Rangers instead. Though now, having seen what happened at Ibrox in recent times, we can look back on it as a near miss. If you believe that you'll believe anything.

It's hard to say why Ayr still mean everything to me. I've spent many more years of my life in Edinburgh than Ayrshire, but neither Hearts nor Hibs do anything for me. I've tried both teams but there's simply nothing there. The fact that I grew up in Prestwick isn't enough. The fact that I was able to share it with my dad is really the reason my connection to the club continues. He never did admit to being an Ayr fan himself, continuing with the illusion that he was a Rangers supporter, but he would still go with me to the games until he reached the stage where he was physically unable. Then I would phone in a quick report after the game. Even after he passed away I still found myself looking for my phone to give him a quick call.

For me the importance of family to football is vital. It's the glue that holds it all together. I've been taking my son and daughter to games since they were toddlers, the way my dad did with me. They've both been to some of the less glamorous grounds in the lower divisions as I tried to convince them that supporting a team that wins every week is not always the best way to appreciate football. Some may call it a football education, others might see it as brainwashing.

They did witness some success, though, as we all watched Ayr win the Second Division in 1997 at Berwick Rangers, but in those days my daughter preferred shouting at the players to get them to wave to her to actually watching the game.

By the early 2000s Ayr looked like they were heading back to the top tier again. Helped by investment from the owner Bill Barr they were building teams that were capable of beating anyone on their day. The attitude had returned. The confidence of McLeod's teams. And they showed this repeatedly in the cup competitions with a succession of wins against Premier League teams including Dundee United, Motherwell, Hibernian and, on a regular basis, our local rivals Kilmarnock. A 3-0 win against Killie was topped off with a glorious Panenka from Andy Walker, who in that moment became an Ayr United legend.

And in 2002 we were in the League Cup semi-final again. This time it was against Hibernian rather than Rangers or

Celtic and an Eddie Annand penalty won the match to take Ayr to their first ever national cup final. Again I cried but what was more significant was that my now Hibs-supporting son was having his own moment of realisation. That season, like many more before, he'd seen Ayr many more times than he'd seen Hibs. He knew all of the Ayr players and very few of the Hibernian ones. He realised he was an Ayr fan.

We lost the final against a Rangers team featuring Tore André Flo, Stefan Kloss, Arthur Numan and Claudio Caniggia and a week later lost a Scottish Cup semi-final to Celtic, but in both games we competed well.

We never managed to reach the Premier League again but maybe the players never quite believed we could as Somerset Road wasn't deemed suitable for the top division at that time. Bill Barr also owned a construction company that was erecting new football grounds all over Scotland and beyond, though he never managed to get local planning permission to build a new ground for Ayr. We still reside in our old-fashioned ground, but to be honest I wouldn't have it any other way.

And now we find ourselves in the third tier of Scottish football trying to match teams such as Stenhousemuir, Forfar and Brechin. Despite this, I still follow the team and still hope for better days. What makes it even better is sharing the pain with my son and daughter who have now both become avid fans. Brainwashing? Maybe. But what also helped has been another personal connection with the club.
My daughter, who is now a sports

science graduate, had never been all that sporty. Despite my best efforts to show her the delights of being an Ayr supporter (we convinced her Ryan Giggs played for us when she was very young) and being taken to a few games at Old Trafford (the last one she spent reading a comic), she had never shown that much interest in football. But during her university studies she started to demonstrate a great interest and enthusiasm for sport science which meant she started following football again. Which obviously meant I could start dragging her along to Ayr games, this time more willingly. The conversations became as much about *the risk factors of soft tissue injuries and sprint technique* as it did the football itself.

And then she saw that the Ayr United Football Academy were looking for some sport science support. She was excited to get involved. I was thrilled. She would be working with future Ayr United stars! And of course this made for an even greater connection with the club for her. Before long she found herself helping the club physio and working with the first team. Actual Ayr United players.

The 2014-15 season had started well after reaching the play-offs the previous year. We were now led by a former player, Mark Roberts, who was still finding his way in management. Three wins in the first three games meant we were sitting top of the league and even after a couple of losses we managed to hold on to the top spot for a few weeks. But things started going wrong. A combination of injuries and a very small squad meant we started losing form and losing games. We were in free-fall. Around this time I received my birthday gift: that signed Ayr top. My daughter, using her new-found access to the first team dressing room, had asked Roberts and his players to sign it. They were bemused. Why would anyone want a signed top from such a team of under-achievers? Well, for me they were still Ayr United players. And hearing what was happening at the club around this time was a real insight into the kind of goings-on that most supporters never get to hear about. My lips were sealed but I felt strangely privileged.

My daughter was quickly learning what life was really like behind the supposed 'glamour' of a 'real' football team. She was also having to adapt quickly to being a young woman in a testosterone-filled environment, but was soon giving as good as she got from players both young and old. To the point that when all the gallows humour about the manager getting sacked was being bandied about she was able to ask him to let her sit in the dug-out on a match-day so she could hear all the abuse first-hand. He promptly invited her to be part of the first-team squad for that weekend's visit to Dunfermline.

So it was that she travelled with the first team, was involved in the warm-up before the game and during half-time. And she sat on the bench. My daughter. Sitting on the Ayr United bench. This was surreal. It was also the start of a run of ten consecutive games I attended hoping to see a win, something I'm not often used to doing living 80 miles away.

Mark Roberts lasted one more game and by the time of the visit to Brechin we had a new manager in the shape of the more experienced Ian McCall. We travelled in a snowstorm to the Angus ground to witness yet another defeat. It was obvious then that changes were happening and my daughter would revert to just being a fan on the terracing again but we continued to go through the weekly anguish of looking for a win. It finally came away to Stirling Albion with a resounding 4-1 victory, but any hope of a resurgence and a climb up the table were soon dashed as we continued our inconsistent form. Indeed only the fact that Stirling Albion were so poor and Stenhousemuir, like us, were a struggling side meant that by the time it came to the last game of the season a win would guarantee third bottom and mean we avoided the play-offs. Unfortunately that game was away from home against a Forfar side trying to win the Championship, but we turned in our best performance of the season to win 3-1 and survive.

The team celebrated as if they'd won the league, which was understandable if a little embarrassing. My daughter and I felt pleased and relieved but oddly disappointed that we weren't going to get to see at least four more games in the play-offs. It had been that kind of season. Awful football at times. Occasionally exciting. Emotional. Yet somehow very personal.

I am no longer able to share the love of my football club with my dad, but this void has been filled by my son and daughter who now have a renewed emotional connection with Ayr United: my daughter from being personally involved for a while with her dad's team and my son seeing his wee sister doing half-time warm-up exercises with our young rising star Alan Forrest.

It had been a long and painful season that had started with us watching a closed-doors 6-1 defeat to our rivals Kilmarnock and ended with Ayr beating one of the league's better teams away from home. And that strip hanging on my office wall will always remind of it.

Whether my son and daughter continue to be Ayr United fans for the rest of their lives remains to be seen, but hopefully this awful season has been the one that will have convinced them. And that makes all pain and anguish worth it, and that signed Ayr United strip a very personal and treasured gift.

This Sporting Half-Life

Sport, ageing and a novelist's grudging acceptance of mortality

By Alex Preston

There's a song by The National — "Mr November" — the refrain of which, both wearily resigned to and furious at the passing of time, repeats: "I used to be carried in the arms of cheerleaders." I saw The National at the American ambassador's party at Winfield House last summer. The band were greying and florid, middle-aged men shuffling about the stage erected above the parquet of a grand entrance hall. When they launched into "Mr November," the ambassador let out a cheer, beamed, explored the liminal space between nodding and headbanging. I bounced my way to the front of the crowd and sang along to that wistful chorus, a note of ironical distance in my voice. How much younger, more vital, less grey-streaked and life-worn I was than those ancient shades on stage, how far from such nostalgic excesses. As they played, I felt my way into their American skins, constructing *Friday Night Lights*-tinted visions of their youthful triumphs, sliding down the lead singer's gristly baritone to floodlit football fields, to home runs that spiralled up, up, up into perfect summer skies, to Ivy League lacrosse games and victorious keg parties in pennant-bedecked dorm rooms.

I left the party, taking a Ferrero Rocher from the pyramid by the front door, and, humming "Mr November" to myself, hailed a cab home. When I got back, on a late-night whim, still slightly drunk on ambassadorial bourbon cocktails, I looked up The National on Wikipedia, and, with creeping Edgar Allen Poe-ish horror, noted their ages. It was as if I'd glanced in the mirror to find myself grey and wizened, my teeth time-filed to stumps. They were my age, you see, and far from some pogoing ingénue at the front of the stage that evening, I'd been part of their melancholy nostalgic construct all along, a balding dad desperately trying to hold off the coming of my middle years. The loss of my youth hit me with a warp-speed whump and, sitting rigid at my kitchen table, I could feel entropy taking place, my consciousness delving down to the cellular level where I was losing battle after microscopic battle. I pulled at the skin of my cheeks, of my throat, checking for the onset of jowls. I ran my hands through what was left of my once-thick locks, looking down to see, clinging to my clammy palms, dozens of strands of hair which had given up the job of adhering to my increasingly visible, cadaverous scalp.

Life is a series of expulsions; some we embrace, others are thrust upon us. Some happen without us even knowing it, and we only recognise the fence that has been erected between and us and some once-familiar place when we try to gain access. As I sat up that night, wallowing in my *crise d'age*, I thought back to my own childhood triumphs, trying to draw a link between the bespectacled, balding schlemiel I'd become and that distant dauphin to whom everything had come easily, sporting success most of all. I saw myself breasting white finishing tapes, felt the weight of trophies, of victores ludorum, of parental and professorial expectation; I remembered sevens tournaments and football cups and cricket tours and always, there in the centre, the gangly boyish figure looking through the curtains of his hair, bewildered at his own facility.

Love first came to me through cricket. Her name was Sally, soft-skinned, white-blonde Sally. Sally sat under trees frothy with blossom at her school – Christ's Hospital – and watched as I knocked off a 50-ball 76 on an early summer day of intense heat and impossibly blue skies. In her uniform – a long black robe with white collar – beside the scorer's hut, she looked like a sexy monk waiting for confession. When I'd finally skied one to mid-on, she was there applauding and, after raising my bat to my teammates, I took her off to some bosky nook and covered her pale tender places with kisses. Even now, walking out to bat for the creaking gaggle of dipsomaniacs with whom I play cricket, I look for Sally on the boundary rope, wonder at the impossible other life in which I'd treated her better, and was still able to kiss that pale, soft skin, to breathe in the scent of her, to have her to felicitate, or more often commiserate, as I took the long walk back to the pavilion.

I wasn't cut out for school. Probably any school, but particularly the one I was at. I'd won a scholarship, otherwise I wouldn't have been there at all, and,

while I believe it's better these days, back then it was populated with the clotted crème de la crème, the sons of belligerent men who'd made fortunes in vinyl flooring and reproduction furniture. The teaching wasn't up to much, my fellow pupils broadly unsympathetic and the sports field was my only escape, a place where I could step outside of my melancholy teenage self, where the overwhelming concerns of being 15 or 16 receded and I was able to live in the moment of movement, in the pure teleology of sport.

It wasn't enough, though, and my year in the fifth, when the 30 or so sixth-form girls were suddenly visible and available, ditto a bitter and lurid amphetamine that was sold under the sobriquet of 'pink champagne', I went off the rails. There was something reckless, wilful in the way I went about ensuring my expulsion. I lived a giddy few months of daring bolts through girls' windows at a duenna's monitory knock, midnight dashes through echoing cloisters lit with sad orange light, sinister assignations at the roundabout by the leisure centre in town. I stayed dutifully sober and slept well on Tuesday and Friday nights, mindful of the exigencies of midweek and weekend sport on the morrow. But otherwise all was excess and subterfuge and the frantic pursuit of the next hedonic hit. Then the allure of unravelling became too much. I was caught and caught again, hauled in front of the head, my housemaster hunched disappointedly beside me. A hard Victorian regimen of 6am cross-country runs and early bedtimes was imposed upon me. I still remember the sponginess of the downland beneath my feet on those aurorean runs, the mist that rose from the fields in the day's first light, the noise of my breath in silent air as I made my solitary way along the long crests of hills.

Then, with preternatural cruelty, the school's powers proscribed the one comfort that had kept me from the dangerous edge of things. I was told that there would be no more sport until my behaviour improved. It was the summer term, and all I'd lived for were nets after supper, the concentrated mindfulness of the well-built innings, the ritualised fallalery of cricket: the pads, the bats, streaks of red on white trousers. Worse still, I was made to score on Saturdays – locked in a dim hut beside some glaucous-skinned pansy to watch my comrades fight on without me. It's a unique form of torture, as a batsman, to see a bowler who fancies himself a bit serve up half-volley after half-volley, the occasional long-hop that just begs to be launched into the lap of some long-necked lower-sixth beauty in front of the pavilion, and to observe the batsman who's taken your place in the order nervously blocking, feathering an ineffectual nudge here, patting respectfully back to the bowler there. I'd duck my head beneath the table and light a frustrated cigarette until the scorer's hut was fogged with smoke, my reluctant companion spluttering and gasping at his Ventolin.

My punishment continued after the summer holidays, which I'd spent in the US playing and watching baseball, getting drunk on South Street in Philly and horrifying my parents by coming home with a tattoo and a pierced ear (the latter removed, the former hidden). Back at school, I was made to run the line in football matches, trotting half-

heartedly alongside the play, rain blurring my vision and soaking my tracksuit. I gave deliberately controversial calls, flagged the opposition offside when they weren't, made myself as refractory and rebarbative as possible. It wasn't just adolescent pique, though. Without sport, I could feel something within me dying: it was like a glass wall had been built between me and my friends, and watching them play a game I loved, watching long limbs chasing down a ball, shaping to shoot, watching the unfettered jouissance of the goal, all of this tied wire around my heart, throttled all that was best and brightest in me. I dreamt of sport, dreams that seemed to dwell only just below the surface, so that I'd wake gripping an imaginary cricket bat or with my duvet kicked to the floor by the churning of frantic feet.

In the end, I gave in. Or rather, I took my sinful proclivities deep underground, buried them in the depths of night, became solitary and shifty where I had once been companionable in my debauchery. I only let myself loose in the wide open spaces of half-term and exeat weekends, when there were no checks on me and I'd run wild in London, clubbing in Soho with a group of attractively disaffected Hampstead kids. We'd go back to their parents' grand houses overlooking the Heath and smoke until dawn. I fell in love with a girl called Jo and we had one of those tragic, secretive, destructive relationships that people write about. She was Sally's dark mirror and we made each other terribly unhappy. Just writing her name makes my heart stretch like it's reaching out for something.

My outward submission to the school's remedial regime worked, though, and in the Lent term I was allowed to play rugby. I remember the joy of walking out onto the field for that first game, at home, under the long arc of a white, heatless, winter sun. I remember the dimpled leather of the ball in my hands and, early on, a gap in the opposition's defence which I made for with that surging, agonised feeling that comes with the prospect of a try or a goal or a six, a feeling that is on the verge of tears and fills the chest and tenses the face. I remember the wind pouring through the sky, the burn of breath in my lungs, the sense of being in a state of selfless, superlative flow.

Whether it was the weeks spent scoring, smoking, trotting apathetically up and down touchlines, I can't now say. All I know is that when I tried to accelerate into that gap, sending out those familiar synaptic commands that had won me so many races, left so many lumpen defenders staring heavenwards, scotched a thousand would-be run-outs, nothing happened. It was like one of those nightmares where the world is rushing by but you're like an oil-soused gull, your limbs monstrous and useless. I felt danger drawing in around me. The gap was closed, the ravenous pack descended, I looked wildly for a teammate to whom I could pass the ball. With the sound of a melon being dropped from height onto a concrete floor, eight or nine of the opposition landed on me. While the rest of me curled into a cowardly ball, one leg was still gamely going for the try line and took most of the force of the hit; it buckled, ligaments twanging and popping like a firing squad taking aim at my sporting life.

They let me out of hospital that night, on crutches, my knee heavily bandaged. It could have been a good deal worse,

the genial doctor said with a chuckle, but you'll be laid up for three months at the very least. I didn't speak to my housemaster as he drove us back from the hospital through the dark and empty suburban streets of Worthing, Sompting, Lancing. I remember the echo of my crutches as I crossed the quadrangle to my house, hobbled unspeakably past those shadowy, sympathetic characters who congregated in the corridors, making each other toast with Marmite and mugs of tea, and into my room. I threw myself down on my bed and sobbed until I felt empty and calm and resigned. I was expelled three days later.

I was about to say that the sportsman in me never recovered from that setback. It was as if I'd somehow adopted the authoritarian association between sport and sin, and was punishing myself for the fuckery and failure. Even when my knee was well-healed, I didn't take up the (distinctly more limited) sporting opportunities at the comprehensive to which I'd been exiled. I played some cricket at Oxford, turned out for my college at football, for the Cowley Cowboys in rugby, but sport had become an afterthought, a snatched pleasure between the more dependable distractions of books and girls and drinking. It was no longer the organising obsession of my life. In London I got fat and bald and could go months without picking up a ball or a racquet or a bat.

It is only since the arrival of what the Germans call *Torschlußpanik* – fear of the shutting door – that sport has gained a poignant, belated importance. It's partly that, as I close in on 40, I feel the melancholy appreciation of the soon-to-be-lost, like the hero of John Cheever's

The Swimmer – "he might have been compared to a summer's day, particularly the last hours of one." It's also that I have found a replacement for those dazzling feats of individual skill, the selfish glories of my youthful game: the love of a team. In cricket, with the Authors XI, and with my gang of 19-year-old toughs in the West London Sunday League (I, a benevolent, and thus-far undroppable, paterfamilias), I have surrounded myself with friends whose triumphs I celebrate as if they were my own, whose joy in my own small successes makes me feel, albeit briefly, as if I were in that nostalgia-drenched song, carried in the arms of cheerleaders.

"You are not Nacka Skoglund!"

The meteoric rise and terrible fall of the Swedish Internazionale legend

By Gunnar Persson

In 1952, Alfredo Foni revolutionised the tactics of Internazionale, turning the team from all-out attack to *catenaccio* and winning their first Scudetto for 13 years. He was able to do this thanks to the genius of one player, Lennart 'Nacka' Skoglund. Despite his success, Foni was dismissed by the club president Carlo Masseroni, who thought he was destroying the game. Inter were not yet ready to win at all costs.

When Foni took charge of Inter in the summer of 1952, he suffered an immediate setback as contract negotiations with the star Dutch forward Faas Wilkes broke down. *Il Tulipano* had enjoyed great individual success in three seasons at Inter. But he was a 29 year old with a dodgy knee. He needed surgery on damaged cartilage, which made the club unwilling to gamble on his future. Opening the knee of a footballer was serious business, with months of rest and rehab ahead before you knew whether he would be able to regain fitness. Foni watched as the crowd favourite signed for Torino and then sat down to figure out how to turn this indisputable loss to his advantage.

In the 1930s, Foni had been a defender of international stature, renowned for his toughness and mental resilience. He replaced Virginio Rosetta at Juventus

in 1934-35 to partner Pietro Rava, just in time for the last of Juve's five consecutive Serie A victories, and played 229 consecutive league games for the club. Foni was an Olympic champion in Berlin in 1936 and a World Cup-winner in 1938, when he and Rava were voted into the team of the tournament.

Bearing this in mind, it was no great surprise when he started erasing attackers from his tactical blackboard. But he also felt he had to do something extraordinary to break the pattern of Serie A, which since the war had been strongly influenced by high-scoring foreign imports. From 1946 onwards the league champions had usually scored more than 100 goals over the 38 games of the season. Torino had shown the way with an incredible 125 in 1947-48. Juventus and Milan accepted the challenge, rather than digging down and kicking the attacking verve out of their opponents, and were ready successors when that great Torino side was wiped out by the Superga diaster in May 1949. Individually, the 35 goals scored by Milan's Swedish tank Gunnar Nordahl in 1949-50 is still a record in the Italian post-war game.

Inter had tried to compete with the other all-out attacking teams in their kind of game. But Inter always fell short. Foni felt there had to be other ways of trying to win, especially if you didn't have a Nordahl or a John Hansen (Juventus) up front. In 1952 there was a change in league format: twenty teams were cut to eighteen; 38 league rounds became 34. A smaller number of games meant every loss counted for more and became more difficult to rectify.

Foni knew what some of his colleagues had done, or had tried to do. Gipo Viani, who took Salernitana to Serie A in 1947, sacrificed an attacker to reinforce the defence. But it didn't work. The pride of Salerno failed to win away and finished last. Nereo Rocco did better in that same season (47-48) with his home town club Triestina. He altered their basic formation along the same lines and finished a more than credible second. Triestina shared that spot with Juventus and Milan, fully 16 points behind the champions Torino. The winners outscored everybody (with a goal difference of 125–33) while Triestina backstopped themselves into second place (51–42). They finished eighth in the two following seasons, but have since never been seen in the top half of Serie A. Neither Salernitana nor Triestina ever seriously challenged for the title. They had only used these tactics to survive. The problem for Foni, managing a big-time club constantly chasing titles and glory, was to find a solution: how could he reinforce the defence by diminishing the attack without losing the ability to win regularly?

For starters he had better players than Salernitana or Triestina, more skilled and abler in the art of counter-attacking. The team that his predecessor Aldo Olivieri had taken to third place in 1951-52 looked like this: Ghezzi; Blason,

Giovannini, Giacomazzi (Padulazzi); Fattori, Neri; Armano, Broccini (Wilkes), Lorenzi, Skoglund, Nyers. Wilkes, plagued by his knee, had lost 15 games to injury, so the team already knew how to cope without him. But Foni went beyond that. He scrapped one of the inside-forward positions altogether. Young Pietro Broccini soon realised he had been pushed way back in the competition for first-team places.

Foni restructured the team completely. The goalkeeper Giorgio 'Kamikaze' Ghezzi remained but Ivano Blason was moved from right-back to become the free defender, the one without a designated opponent who would always be able to support his colleagues. The journalist Gianni Brera, one of the few who appreciated what Foni was doing, described how Blason added qualities to the team, especially after a couple of minutes defending: "...then, suddenly, Blason fires a bombshell from deep within his own half, and 70 metres away you will not find many opponents, only wide open spaces exploitable for the great skilled individualists of Internazionale."

Gino Armano was drawn back from outside-right to right-back and added further precision to this counter-attacking long-ball game. The centre-half Attilio Giovannini became a stopper who now knew he could choose between making a risky tackle or just anticipating and irritating, as Blason always was there to cover and support him. The left-back Silvano Giacomazzi retained his position.

In the process Foni created a new entity, a well-populated midfield, a purely defensive one acting as a bulwark in front of the defenders. Maino Neri remained, now moved to the right. Bruno Mazza, an acquisition from Legnano, and Fulvio Nesti, a ferocious tackler with remarkable endurance who had joined from SPAL in Ferrara that summer, made up a hard-working trio.

Up front Foni had the three main reasons for his revolution, his three stars capable of entertaining the full defensive force of most opponents.

Benito Lorenzi, nicknamed 'Il Veleno' (Poison), was the mobile and quick central striker. He was on the small side (169 cm/68 kg) and made from a different mould than the powerful Gunnar Nordahl (180/97) or the rangy John Hansen (183/78). Lorenzi was cut out for counter-attacking and obnoxiously effective. He began playing with his home-town club, the amateurs US Borgo a Buggiano, who sold him to Empoli in 1946 for 100,000 lire. A year later Internazionale showed interest, but had to pay 12 million lire to get him. He had been their first-choice striker since. His nickname had nothing to do with football. It was given to him by his mother when he was a boy and plundered the family bakery to share the bread with friends of lesser means.

Stefano Nyers was a fast left-sided attacker, physically compact with an explosive left foot. He had a chequered background. Born István Nyers in Freyming-Merlebach, France, in 1924 to Hungarian parents (his father was a miner), he grew up in Budapest. He was nurtured by III.Kerület and got a chance to play professionally at only seventeen with Szabadkai Vasutas AC in Subotica, Serbia, a territory annexed by Hungary during the Second World War. Then he played briefly alongside László Kubala at Ganz TE before moving across Budapest to Újpesti TE. He left Hungary in 1946, still only 22 years old. After a short stint with Viktoria Zizkov in Prague he went on to Paris. At Stade Français he was coached by a certain Helenio Herrera. He made such an impression in a friendly against Inter in 1948 that the Italians simply had to get him.

Inter had seven defenders and a two-man attack lopsided to the left, with the right-back Armano coming up whenever he had an opportunity. The tenth and last piece of this jigsaw puzzle was the remaining inside-forward, the Swede Lennart 'Nacka' Skoglund, who was a player of wonderful skills, able to trap any hoof from his own defenders. He was the creative mind, the hub Foni needed to get the attack going. In this context, as a modern number 10, Skoglund was as important to Inter as Diego Maradona would be to Napoli 35 years later.

His rise to stardom was rapid. He grew up in Stockholm, not far from the Hammarby headquarters, and made his debut for the club at 16, in 1946. He left them, then a third-division outfit, late in 1949 to join AIK. Swedish football was amateur at the time (until 1967) and quarantine rules (instead of transfer fees) meant he would not be eligible to play a league game until July of the following year. But he could play friendlies and joined the squad for a post-season tour of England. There, at Highbury, the teenager was spotted by another promising youngster, Brian Glanville.

"By chance, I was probably the first journalist to write about him in a London newspaper," Glanville told me a couple of years ago when I was writing Skoglund's biography. "Coincidence was the word, but you didn't need great perception to notice and admire his talents that chilly evening at Highbury. AIK were tired at the end of their tour and got beat badly. Still, the best player on the pitch was a boyish little inside-left with glowing blond hair. His name was Skoglund. I have never seen anything like it, not before or since." Arsenal won the game 8–0.

During the winter Skoglund began his compulsory military service as an artillery gunner at Vaxholm, east of Stockholm. Then he got a lucky break. He was called up late to fill a vacancy when a team picked by the press played the national team as a preparation for the World Cup in Brazil. The cheeky Skoglund showed no respect and scored the two first goals as the Press XI won the game 3–1. At the banquet afterwards he was told to get the necessary vaccinations.

The Yorkshireman George Raynor, who coached both AIK and Sweden, had watched him closely that spring and knew exactly what he was getting, even though Skoglund had yet to play a first division game. The youngster, who had turned 20 on Christmas Eve, went straight into the team for the last friendly, against the Netherlands. He then kept his place for the World Cup opener, in which Sweden faced Italy. Skoglund practically went straight from reserve-team football to the World Cup and wasn't in top shape. But inspiration and good support from the industrious left-half Ingvar Gärd carried him. Sweden won 3–1 against the depleted Italians, who were rebuilding after the Superga disaster a year earlier. Inter put him on their list

and began discussions on the spot. Good for Skoglund, who began to wane during the next game, against Paraguay, and ultimately lost his place after the disastrous 7-1 defeat to Brazil.

He wasn't fit enough and he had also lost focus during the long periods of inactivity between games. The local press named him *Cabelo de Milho* (corn hair) and he got all the attention he wanted at Copacabana. Sometimes Raynor and the team manager Putte Kock had no idea where he was.

Rumours surrounded the squad on the return to Sweden. Eight players had gone abroad after the Olympic victory in London 1948. Within weeks of the World Cup they were followed by a further eleven. Skoglund had to go back to Vaxholm to finish his military service, and became the 20th Swedish player to move abroad when he left in early October.

Carlo (or Charles) Davies went to Stockholm in late August. Davies, the son of AC Milan's charter member Samuel Richard Davies, was responsible for recruiting new players to Inter and he was determined to get this one. The first 19 Swedes to move had been paid between 75,000 and 130,000 kronor for their signatures. Davies offered 120,000. Skoglund replied, whimsically, "Oh, I have another offer of 140,000." The negotiation went on and they finally reached an agreement at 165,000. When it came to signing, he realised he still wasn't of age; his 21st birthday was four months away. He called his father Josef, who had to get a taxi to Hotel Reisen in the Old Town and pen his name. 165,000 kronor was a full year's pay for 25 skilled workers.

Nacka Skoglund became a professional and as such he was barred from playing in Sweden. AIK weren't too unhappy to let him go, as he had been alarmingly disinterested during his last few weeks at the club. Besides, AIK had only been able to use him in five league games and a victorious cup final. Losing two mature players was much worse. The wing-half Sune Andersson went to Roma and the striker Bror Mellberg to Genoa. Those were heavy blows and in the end it meant relegation in the spring of 1951.

Skoglund left Sweden five weeks after signing his contract. He flew to Zurich and then headed for Milan by train. He was pulled off at Como by Carlo Davies, to avoid havoc at the final destination. The city of Milan was a revelation to Skoglund. He suddenly had all the money he could ask for, he got a flat at 8 Via Morrone, behind La Scala, and soon found his way to the nightclubs. His habits worried the club management until, in the summer of 1952, he began dating Nuccia Zirelli, a local beauty queen with Calabrian roots. The couple married in early August and his settling into family life, with their first child expected in May 1953, coincided with the appointment of Foni as coach of Inter.

The team got off to a good start and were unbeaten well into the new year. In his first autobiography Nacka recounts the away game against SPAL: "It looked as if we would only get a draw. As usual it was safety first, with only three attackers. It was Nyers, Lorenzi and myself. We ran like poisoned rats, puffing and panting with our tongues hanging out like red ties. 'I can't take this anymore,' complained Lorenzi with five minutes to go. 'Why don't you score a goal?' he

suggested. 'Of course, as you please. But I will wait a minute or two, just to make it more worthwhile.' I told him that just for fun, because I was so exhausted I almost felt sick when I saw the ball. But suddenly I got a good pass from Nyers. I used my last resources to make a dash for it, dribbled past two opponents and hit. It was a blast, like a rocket past their goalkeeper high up in the net."

Inter did not lose until the 20th game, 3-1 against Torino, Faas Wilkes scoring one of the goals. His bad knee restricted him to only 12 games and this was the Dutchman's only goal of the season. Inter lost two more matches before the league title was secured, with a 3-0 win at home against Palermo in the 31st round. Nyers converted a penalty before half time, Skoglund scored the second and Nyers finished with a cannonball. The Inter players were instantly rewarded with a million lire each – and lost the three remaining games.

Inter won the league two points ahead of Juventus. It was a long-awaited reward for the rubber industrialist Carlo Masseroni, who celebrated a decade as club president. Masseroni was happy, but he was also fed up. He had listened to too many remarks during the season. Opposing attackers were drawn into the Inter defensive trawl, where they were outnumbered and inevitably got lost. This was an ugly kind of football, previously unheard of among the top teams of the league. Masseroni was not prepared to take any more of this and simply ordered his coach, "Play like everybody else. At least try to play beautiful football."

You only have to study the league table to see what Masseroni was after. Inter had won. But they had not scored a century of goals, which might have been expected. The goal difference was 46–24. Not a lot to shout about if you were president of a sports club that strived to provide entertainment.

Foni had to comply for the following season. He reverted to a regular 3–2–2–3 – and won again. He used the same players and probably did as he pleased, employing the defensive formation against the top teams and attacking more intensely against the lesser sides. The *catenaccio* genie was out of the bottle anyhow and there was no turning back for football as a sport. This time around Inter took four more points (51), scored more goals (67) and loosened up a bit defensively (32). Foni stayed on for one more year and left the club to become coach of the Italy national team at the same time as Masseroni relinquished the presidency.

The petroleum magnate Angelo Moratti took over and initially had to oversee the break-up of a great team. Moratti liked Skoglund a lot, so much that in 1958 he changed his mind and kept him for a year longer than had been planned. Skoglund had, for some reason, teamed up with Gino Anzanello, the business adviser who had squandered the savings of Stefano Nyers. Anzanello had invested the Hungarian's money in a men's shop that never made profit. The first project with Skoglund was a perfume shop for Nuccia, opened in 1955 but hopelessly located in a back street and abandoned after two years. The second was a bar, even farther away from the town centre at Via Paolo Sarpi. This venture went reasonably, well enough for Anzanello to stick around.

Skoglund left for Sweden in May 1958 to play in the World Cup. To make things easy for Nuccia, he had signed a number of blank cheques. Anzanello got wind of this and made a proposal, to loan the family capital – the savings from eight years as a professional player – to help one of his friends set up a knitting factory. "You will have every penny restored by the time Lennart gets back from Sweden. There will even be interest on top of it."

It seemed a good idea. Nuccia gave Anzanello a cheque with Lennart's signature, and off he went. When Nacka returned to Italy with a silver medal he found his gold was all gone. On top of it he had to go to hospital for a hernia operation. Moratti, whose original intention had been to let Skoglund loose after the World Cup, changed his mind. He presented him with a bonus of 10,000 kronor and also gave him a generous loan to allow him to get on with his life. During his final season at Inter, Skoglund shared his position (now outside-left) with Mario Corso, an enigmatic youngster who soon became the new presidential favourite.

Skoglund left Internazionale in 1959, after nine years, for Sampdoria. Moratti concluded a long search for the right coach in 1960, when Helenio Herrera was sacked by Barcelona. Herrera was a *catenaccio* man, applying the same tactics that Foni had had to give up. In the process he made Inter a team that would win at all costs.

Skoglund spent three seasons with Sampdoria. The team was largely made up of veterans who only got paid when they actually played. The pressure to be selected to earn money and ignore nagging injuries made them use painkillers. Skoglund, who still had his family in Milan, lived the life of a bachelor and began abusing both pills and alcohol. He rounded off his Italian tenure with a disastrous season at Palermo before returning to Sweden.

Nuccia and his two sons stayed in Milan and after a few years the separation became official. He played for Hammarby for four seasons, from 1964 to 1967. He showed glimpses of greatness, as when he scored with a corner kick only minutes into his comeback game against Karlstad. The club made many efforts to find him a job. He tried to sell cars, carpets, books – you name it. Before going to Italy he had been unwilling to work. He never held a job for more than a month or two. This time he was completely unable to adjust to a regular life. He became increasingly irrational. At one point he lived a few blocks from the Hammarby clubhouse but still refused to go there and get on the bus for away games. The bus had to stop outside his door and wait for him. He usually opened the window and shouted, "Got home late yesterday, going into the shower now!" In the end, in 1968, he was kicked out by the fourth-division side Kärrtorps IK, a team coached and managed by his older brother Georg. From then on it was downhill all the way.

Lennart Skoglund became a recluse, fluctuating between bad days and horrible ones; he only went out after dark. One evening he went to an Italian restaurant. It was a quiet place and he made no fuss at all. The waiter became interested and asked how he knew so much about the food and wine on the menu. "Well, I lived and worked in Italy for quite a few years," replied Skoglund. "Really? Doing what?" Perhaps he felt he had said too much when he admitted to have been a professional footballer. "My name is Nacka Skoglund." At this point he was past forty. He had become pudgy and balding. The waiter simply didn't believe what he heard. "Hey, me and dad used to go to the San Siro and watch Inter. You are NOT Nacka Skoglund!" He left the place devastated.

Skoglund's life ended dramatically in his childhood home at Södermalm in Stockholm. One summer night in July 1975 he felt something strange inside him. He panicked rather than call an ambulance. He was found in bed, seemingly asleep, with everything around him turned upside down. He had been suffering a haemorrhage in his abdomen.

Eleven years later the Swedish filmmaker Tom Alandh made a documentary dissecting the tragedy of Skoglund. Most of his old pals were still around. Alandh also went to Milan, where he interviewed Benito Lorenzi. *Il Veleno* was comfortable in front of the camera, speaking Italian and not being pushed into using English. Lorenzi wanted to explain how things were thirty-odd years ago. But he wasn't able to handle the situation emotionally. It was as if he for the first time realised how important his old friend had been for his own success. No words could describe what he felt. All he could give was tears. He cried out of gratitude. Ⓑ

Football v Alzheimer's

How football is being used stimulate the memories of Alzheimer's patients

By Dermot Corrigan

A smile of recognition slowly spreads across the elderly man's face.

"A great goal by Cruyff against Reina," he says, in a voice which strengthens with increasing conviction. "Great cross from the right. And then — with his instep."

"His instep," the man repeats, gesturing with his fingers and now smiling broadly as he remembers the famous back-post volley scored by Johan Cruyff for Barcelona past the Atlético Madrid goalkeeper Miguel Reina in December 1973.

More than four decades on from that goal at the Camp Nou, the lifelong Barça fan is one of a group of patients with Alzheimer's disease who are flicking through the pages of specially produced editions of the Spanish football magazine *Líbero*.

The patients are being helped by a project called *Fútbol v Alzheimer* organised by the Madrid-based *Líbero* and the Universidad Autònoma de Barcelona.

The idea for the project came from a 2014 study produced at the university's Fundació Salut i Envelliment (Foundation Health and Ageing; FSiE). This research found that talking about football helped stimulate the memory, attention and mood of people with Alzheimer's and other forms of cognitive deterioration.

Líbero got in touch with the study's authors, Laura Coll and Sara Domènech, and together they decided to create editions of the magazine that can be used a tool to help during therapy sessions.

Four specially produced editions have as cover stars the legends László Kubala, Alfredo Di Stéfano, Pelé and Cruyff. Each issue includes short articles featuring key games and big personalities from across the decades, alongside specially designed exercises to help stimulate a patient's memory.

"There is one magazine for each age group of patients," *Líbero's* editor Diego Barcala told *The Blizzard*. "One magazine each with contents from the 1940s, 1950s, 1960s and 1970s. They don't have long stories or anything, it's not really a magazine to read or a 'retro' magazine. The contents have medical utility. We worked with the doctors on exercises they use for memory, where the patient must repeat a sequence. Instead of the usual objects, there are footballers. We adapt football content to Alzheimer's exercises so they are useful for the patients."

One page in the 1970s magazine shows the faces of six former players and patients are asked which of the men never played for Barcelona. During the therapy session, a different man spots the former Real Madrid midfielder Vicente Del Bosque in the bottom row of the photo. "It's this one – this is Del Bosque," he says, evidently proud of working it out, and not being foxed by the Spain coach having been photoshopped into a *blaugrana* jersey.

"Alzheimer's erases memories," says Coll, principal investigator at the FsiE, in an especially moving video showcasing the project, which was produced by *Líbero* and the Madrid-based advertising agency LOLA. "It does not erase the passion for football, nor the emotions, and that is what we want to recover using this therapy."

"Things go out of our heads," says a female patient in the video. "But if we see them, we remember."

Líbero is an independent Spanish football magazine launched in June 2012. Barcala says the publication offers an alternative to the mainstream Spanish sports media's fascination with Cristiano Ronaldo's underpants and Lionel Messi's tax affairs.

"One of our ways of being different is our social and political engagement," Barcala said. "We always look to use football to help society, to help people, so that football actually does something. Not just business, money, entertainment. But to help people. Besides the *Fútbol vs Alzheimer* project, we have looked at issues like homophobia in football. All the proceeds from one issue were donated to refugees in Gaza via the UN. We always want football to form part of a social message. We did not want just to do a magazine story - but actually to contribute something."

Barcala said putting together the special magazines meant thinking about how people consumed football decades back, long before 24/7 coverage on the internet or every game live on pay TV.

"The type of football fan which exists now, didn't exist back then," he says. "In those days you couldn't see all the games. Today you can have a fan in Saudi Arabia who knows all about Leo Messi. But in those times, apart from the big stars like Pelé, fans in Spain just saw the team from their own city or big stars like Di Stéfano or Kubala. But they're more connected to their own team which won La Liga in 1946 or remember a particular historic game. Because in the end the emotions of each person are closely connected to their own team."

The project was made public last June and Barcala says the response since has been terrific.

"It's impressive, and surprising, how many people have been in touch," he says. "I've had hundreds of emails, including from many patients' centres which have used football as an impressive way of getting to people's emotions. We also received emails from people who had suffered a lot, situations where their father did not recognise them. They had shared memories of football and could speak about football, even though they did not recognise their own son. That has happened to us a lot. We have received hundreds of emails."

Barcala stressed that the project was not going to 'cure' or provide any long-lasting relief for patients who are suffering from Alzheimer's or other forms of cognitive deterioration.

"Football is not going to help them get their memory back," Barcala says. "It's not about that. What they can recover are their emotions. It's almost more useful for the family members than for the patients. For example, a 30-year-old guy wrote to me saying his granddad could not remember his name, which was very difficult for him to take. But if he played the start of the Atlético Madrid club anthem, his granddad could still finish off the verses. He's not able to remember a face, but can share a moment of emotion around the team. The project is like that too – when family members can recover some big moments, with their father, their granddad. Their families have this frustration, that they cannot interact, but by using football they cry, they laugh, they jump, they shout, they talk and have conversations, it's marvellous."

The *Fútbol v Alzheimer* project has so far not received any public funding or corporate sponsorship, and *Líbero* is not a business with the resources to fund a big print run or PR splash.

However anyone anywhere in the world can go online [http://futbolvsalzheimer. revistaLibero.com] and make a small donation – and if they wish they can nominate the medical centre where they would like the special magazines sent.

"Many people have asked where they can buy these magazines," Barcala said. "But this is not a business move by us. We do not want to sell them for €5. That is why we just ask for a €2 donation for each magazine, as we believe that covers the printing and delivery costs, or €10 for four magazines so they go to a clinic."

The next step in the project will allow people to create their own edition of the magazine online, selecting relevant photos, dates and details, then download it as a PDF or similar file for use with their own relations, friends or neighbours.

"You can put into the website that you are from Valencia, my granddad is 70 years old, his decade is the 1960s," Barcala said. "Then you can download onto a tablet or laptop a free personalised magazine."

Líbero also have plans for using other types of archive material in new ways to produce useful therapeutic tools to help patients.

"We're planning to make podcasts where you can listen to the commentary from games in the 1950s," Barcala says. "We have other ideas too. Because football, in the end, has so much historical content that you can use. The commentators were always the same, their voices are very identifiable for the patients. Maybe for the Spain team at the World Cup or Madrid in the European Cup. All the games were not televised then, people listened on their local radio stations."

Barcala says he and the University of Barcelona are keen to investigate different ways in which patients or clinics in other countries can be aided. There is no shortage of ideas – and there is a possibility that clubs or players might be interested in helping out.

"Colo-Colo, from Chile, wrote to us to say they wanted to get involved," he says. "Juan Pablo Sorín, the ex-footballer, also got in touch to ask how he could participate."

The *Fútbol v Alzheimer* project really does seem to be a pretty rare example of football really being used to help people just for that reason, not as a by-product of a project with a different ultimate aim or a roundabout way of trying to sell something to somebody.

Even if you don't understand Spanish the video – at *http://bit.ly/blzzrd19* – packs a lot more emotional punch than any 21st century multi-million dollar budget boot advert or slow-motion post-game action montage.

"It's nice to remember the good things," one elderly patient says at its close. "The bad things, I forget. But the good things are nice."

In the UK, footballmemories.org.uk, set up by Alzheimer's Scotland, is also using football to help Alzheimer's sufferers. Ⓑ

75

Interview

"He came home angry once because
his dog was quicker than him."

The Throwback

Robert Lewandowski is proving the value of the old-fashioned striker. But what created him?

By Maciej Iwanski

The winter is severe in Warsaw. It is 14 January 2006. Robert Lewandowski is seventeen, with a head full of dreams of becoming the next star of Legia Warsaw's attack. He is tall and slim and arrived just a few months ago from Legia's small satellite club in the fourth division, Delta. After signing a one-year deal with Legia, he was immediately sent to play for the reserves in the third division. On this particular day, it's five degrees below zero, and the snow is piled around the artificial grass pitch where Legia reserves play in the Syrenka Cup, a friendly tournament, against other local teams from lower divisions. In the final, Legia face their local rivals, Polonia. Lewandowski scores five.

"I don't really remember that match," Lewandowski said nine years later, shortly after captaining Poland to a place at Euro 2016 and finishing the qualifiers as top scorer. Poland secured qualification for France at the super-modern Stadion Narodowy, 8km away from Legia's old ground. "Well, I do remember the pitch we played at and that it took a while to adapt to the conditions," he recalls. "I can't believe what happened." He scored his first goal in the second minute, with the others coming in the 5th, 9th, 12th and 34th. Legia's reserves won the Syrenka Cup, but it was the only silverware they lifted with Lewandowski in the team. A few weeks later he was injured – the only serious injury he has ever had – and after treatment he was sold for £1000 to another third division team, Znicz Pruszków. It's a mistake Legia fans regret to this day. To be fair the club, though, even Lewandowski's most devout fan couldn't have predicted what a player he would become.

"I'll never agree with those who claim my son was meant for football," Lewandowski's mother, Iwona, said. She saved his career. "I remember that day as if it had happened yesterday. He was at the end of his break, ready to come back and fight for his chance at best club in our region. I was waiting in the car and I immediately saw something was wrong. He was devastated: 'Mama, they erased me from their plans. It's over.' I simply couldn't believe it." Even all these years later, she is clearly moved by the memory. "We came back home. I made the dinner. He refused to eat. I didn't know what to do. And suddenly, I decided to call one of his previous coaches and ordered Robert to get his boots. We drove to meet him and he immediately called Znicz. Within 40 minutes we were there. Their team was getting ready for training. The coach came in and saw Robert. He knew him from Legia. 'What the hell?!' he shouted. 'Get yourself ready for training now!'

Robert was so happy when he heard this. It was the beginning of a new era."

Iwona Lewandowski smiled and stopped for a little while. We met in a brand new sushi restaurant in central Warsaw and talked for more than two hours. She came with her other child, Robert's sister, Milena, who is three years his elder. At that moment Milena and I looked at Iwona as her strong, joyful voice started to waver. I noticed that her brown eyes were in tears. "I've no idea why I'm acting like this," she said. "This was never me. I did it all the way my husband would have done it. I believe he pushed me from heaven to help our only son. Krzys passed away in March 2005. I never realised before, but yes, he never saw Robert playing professional football even once. But it was he who shaped the man Robert is now."

Lewandowski was raised in a family in which sport was as natural as breathing. Iwona represented Poland at volleyball; Krzysztof was a European junior champion in judo. He was the one who decided their son's name. "He knew we were going to raise a footballer. That's why he is Robert: travelling through Europe Krzysztof witnessed how important it would be to have an internationally recognisable name."

When Robert was eight, he lived in Leszno, 30km and 40 minutes by bus from Warsaw. His father taught him judo, but decided his body was much more suited for football. But the basics of martial arts would be very useful years later, when Robert fights with defenders. The local club Partyzant had no junior teams, so Robert needed to go to Varsovia, where he trained and played with boys two years older. "He was small and very slim, but he knew what to do," his sister says. "Sport was everything to us. I trained to play volleyball so our parents were a little bit stretched. It was normal that I had to wait two or three hours until Robert was finished, or the opposite. And of course, we played matches on weekdays."

Milena is the charming and beautiful mother of Leon, a six-month-old boy sleeping in the stroller next to our table. With her husband, Radek, she runs a bespoke tailor shop called Signor Leone. Robert, who refuses to confirm if he invested his money in the family business, wears their suits. "Yeah, it's really quality stuff," Robert says. "And Radek is very professional. He needed only two hours to work on me; he never asked me back again like others did."

Officially, Robert's first club was Varsovia. Although he started playing football when he was six at Partyzant Leszno, they never registered him. They regret this now, as Uefa transfer rules would have earned them enough money to survive for years after his moves to Borussia Dortmund and Bayern Munich. But it's not that Lewandowski never played for Partyzant. Despite playing basketball, volleyball, handball (always in the school's first team) and running, he operated under a false name. In one of the matches he scored a few goals and at half-time his father and coach decided to substitute him so that their opponents would not start checking the documents. Milena treats this as a joke. "I think this is the most crazy thing my little brother did in his all life," she she laughs.

But that's not true. "Robert told me that when he was a teenager he took his parents' car once and went away somewhere," Wojtiech Zawiola, a journalist for Polish broadcaster nc+ claims. But Lewandowski is not the kind of man who would seek trouble. "We had warm, loving home," Iwona says. "We gave him confidence, protected his education and tried to help him develop as the footballer. It was his dream from the very first moment of his life, and also his father's dream. Especially Legia. Krzys was huge fan of the club."

Lewandowski was 16 when his parents decided it was time for the kids to move to Warsaw. So, Robert had only one bus instead of two hours driving for every training session and every match at Varsovia. He lived with his sister in a small apartment owned by the family. The parents came as often as they could. Robert asked his father to video training and matches, so they could watch them and correct any mistakes. He also competed against his dog. "He came home angry once," Iwona remembers, "because his dog was quicker than him. He tried to be faster until he succeeded. I laughed, but now I see that he was focused on winning, always and everywhere. It wasn't easy, and he was much smaller than the other kids."

"We had to work a lot on him, but he was a pure talent," Krzysztof Sikorski, Lewandowski's first coach at Varsovia, told the TVP cameras after his protégé had hit five in nine minutes after coming off the bench at half-time against Wolfsburg in the Bundesliga in September 2015. "He loved football and the ball loved him." He likes to tell the story of the end of the 1999 season, when Lewandowski

wasted six one-on-one chances in a game and the team lost 1-0. "The other boys were so used to Robert scoring that nobody ran forward to help him," Iwona remembers. "He was devastated until next match when he scored again.

"And Varsovia were very poor — they couldn't afford respectable facilities. He changed in the backseat of our car and I always came with sausage and bread after the match, but when he scored he could eat his beloved muffins. Something his wife would now kill him for." All three of us laugh.

Robert was 16 when his father died. "Robert didn't really have time to see this," said Milena. "I was older, and we decided with Mama that I would be the one knowing what was going on. He passed away very rapidly. Robert was obviously very moved by this. He never talked with Tata about his disease, but he felt the shadow that was coming."

Then it was time to sort out Robert's next move. He and his family chose Delta, Legia satellite club. On 30 April 2005, in front of 200 spectators, Robert scored his first senior goal, against KS Łomianki in the fourth division, on a small pitch with no seats and no stands. After nine months he decided it was time to move to Legia, as the financially troubled Delta senior team were liquidated. "During the next year, he never received any real chance at Legia," Iwona remembers. "I remember that watching the reserve-team matches many people asked why Robert never got a chance." Legia seemed to prefer a forward called Dawid Janczyk.

The knee injury ended his hopes at Legia. "Robert was so energetic that I couldn't stand him when he was injured," Milena said, shaking her head. "I was happier than my brother when he could get back to playing. But not for Legia."

Janczyk signed for Legia in 2005, and two years later was sold to CSKA Moscow for more than €4m. After scoring only twice and being loaned to four clubs he was sold to Piast Gliwice in 2014. After a year there he is without a club and almost out of football, admitting he has disciplinary problems.

Robert shows no sign of bitterness about what happened at Legia. He's very different from the shy boy I met in 2007 when he was at Znicz and I was working as a commentator for TVP, covering second-division games. Lewandowski was the lethal weapon of the youngest team, the newcomers who nearly made it to the top flight. Eight years on he's a gladiator, a European star and the captain of the national team. But I still get the impression every time we talk that he's pretty much the same boy, focused on team winning.

"The injury I had during the year I was there was the reason Legia did not believe in my future," Lewandowski said. "I was only a reserve-team prospect then, but that was not the future written for me. It was a painful experience, but only for a moment."

Lewandowski graduated from high school and enrolled as a student at Warsaw's Academy of Physical Education, where his parents met more than two decades ago. It's there that he met Anna, a karate champion and future

world champion with the Poland national team. He introduced himself as Andrzej. He was in a group, sure she would not remember his name, so he didn't care. The next time they met she called him by his false name. Surprised she knew it, Robert started talking to her.

At that time in the third division he earned £230 a month. "I remember that he was driving a blue Fiat Bravo, and he always came to the club with two or three other players so they would share petrol costs," said Leszek Ojrzyński, then the coach of Znicz. Lewandowski remains faithful to Italian cars, driving a red Ferrari, bought after signing his contract with Bayern.

When a friend asked me to set up the meeting with Lewandowski to show him his KTM X-Bow, I texted him — "Wanna ride KTM? 240 horse power, 800 kilos, no roof?" "Sure, let's meet before the national team match," he replied.

We came on the Tuesday, as I knew Robert wanted to stop his activities – interviews, commercial appearances etc – three days before the game. Did he enjoy the ride? "Nice, fast. But I already have a car," he replied. Typical Lewandowski. It's not the money — he earns €100,000 in three days. But he doesn't like to spend when it's not necessary, even though cars are his true passion.

Seven years ago he couldn't even dream about this sort of money. "Robert came to us in the autumn," said Ojrzyński. "He was physically weak, scored three times. After eleven weeks of the winter break, when we could prepare him, he scored twelve goals and we got promoted. In the first division he started scoring and assisting from the very first moment. When I moved to Wisła Płock I wanted to sign him, but he was already priced at £200,000. We couldn't afford him. Maybe it was good, because at Płock he would never have developed as he did at Lech Poznań."

It was at Znicz that Lewandowski started to become recognisable beyond the Warsaw football environment. As he was failing to make it at Legia, the forward Cezary Kucharski was finishing his playing career at the club. "I didn't know him at that time," he said. "The first time I saw him was training at Znicz, where I'd gone to help another player. But when I saw Robert's movement and the touch, I immediately decided to contact him."

We met in Warsaw, in the prestigious modern apartment that serves as CK Sport Management's headquarters. The inside is luxurious and stylish. Kucharski's office has a big brown leather chair and wooden furniture, full of his career football shirts and honours. "In 2006," Kucharski recalls, "I said in an interview that I would stay in football as a players' agent. And that I wanted to raise another David Beckham. I was sure we had that kind of player in Poland; it's just that nobody takes the right care of them. And I knew I wanted to build a big, international career when I found a suitable player. I was lucky to find him right after." Kucharski, who invested the money he made in football into 27 apartments in Warsaw and was elected to Polish parliament, pours a cup of black tea.

He was the first agent to talk to Lewandowski. "Cezary called Robert and when we met I was charmed," said Iwona. "He seemed trustworthy, saying he thought that my son was a future star and had the potential to make a good career abroad. I was touched with the way he talked, promising to help Robert, not just earn from him."

Lewandowski, whose role model was Thierry Henry, liked the prospect of major football abroad. "His first question was, 'What and how should I improve?'" remembers Kucharski. "Well, at that time, despite his huge talent, it was pretty much everything."

By then, Lewandowski could already have been a player at IL Hødd, but the club promoted to Norway's top flight never sent an official transfer request. They decided that a player from the Polish third division was too much risk. When Kucharski came on the scene, Lewandowski was on his way to becoming the second division's top scorer, as he had been the previous season in the third. The offers started to come. "Half of the Ekstraklasa teams wanted Robert," Kucharski said. The choice seemed obvious: Legia.

At that time, Legia were a superpower waiting to be born. With a new rich owner the future seemed bright. Mirosław Trzeciak, their sports director and a former national-team forward, had been searching for a new striker. As the man who scored the winning goal in Osasuna's crucial match while battling for promotion to La Liga, Trzeciak was taken by the idea of signing a player from Spain rather than giving a chance to a promising Pole. One day the mobile phone of Znicz Pruszków's president Sylwiusz Mucha-Orliński rang: "Trzeciak here. You can sell Lewandowski, we just signed Mikel Arruabarrena. In this situation your boy would be fifth in line to play at Legia." Arruabarrena failed in Poland and Lewandowski signed for Legia's biggest rivals, Lech Poznań. Robert was not to fulfil his father's dream of being a star in the city of his birth.

Seven years later, Kucharski claims Legia had no chance. "I was the one who told Robert, 'You should not go to Legia.' Why? Because I was captain at that club and I knew they were not going in the right direction at that time. Lech gave us the chance of moving forward, up to the title. The coach Franciszek Smuda wanted my player and from the very first moment we all felt this was the right thing to do." What Kucharski does not say is that Lech's offer was not the best one. But Znicz's president, grateful for what Lewandowski had achieved, told the player he would agree to any transfer suitable for Robert, as he signed him for almost nothing. Lech payed £200,000 plus bonuses. In other words, Lewy was worth a million złoty. And he signed the first deal that made him a rich man – his basic salary was £8,000 a month. One of his first decisions was helping his mother buy a new car, which for Robert has become a relative common expenditure.

In Poznań, one of Poland's biggest cities, only a 90-minute drive to Berlin thanks to new A2 motorway, Lech means everything. The city breathes the club. Fans were delighted with the signing of Lewandowski. "It was extremely important to us," Kucharski said. "Every coach offered a place in the first team from the start, but Lech's stadium, under construction before Euro 2012,

with passionate fans, helped us prepare for the next move. When we were negotiating terms, I already told Lech's owner that we were going there to win something and take another step."

"We decided to sign Robert Lewandowski after deep research made by our Scouting Department," explained Piotr Rutkowski, vice-president and son of the owner, Germany-based businessman Jacek Rutkowski. "We observed him many times and wanted to know everything about him. He was getting better and better every day, and very soon foreign clubs started asking about him."

If their research was so good, though, why didn't Smuda know anything about Robert's personal life? "Cezary asked me once to drive with him to Białystok, where Lech were playing Jagiellonia in a league match the next day," said Iwona. "We met the coach in the hotel lobby. He knew nothing about Robert's father and all that story. Maybe he didn't care. But after that he said in an interview that he knew Robert would never cause any trouble and would keep his feet on the ground."

Smuda is linked with another story. Watching one of the Znicz matches to scout Lewandowski he decided to leave early, dismissing the forward. "Are you crazy?" he shouted at Kucharski so everybody in the small VIP area in Pruszków could hear. "What is this? A boy with wooden legs? Give me back the money I spent on petrol."

"Yeah, that was fun," said Kucharski as he poured another cup of tea. "It was all a set-up. Smuda went crazy about Lewandowski. But he knew other coaches might do the same. So he asked me if he could leave early and shout at me. I was surprised at that moment, but played my role and few minutes later he assured me this was only an act for other club's representatives watching Robert." The story is good, but local journalists claim Smuda would have preferred the experienced Tomasz Frankowski over Lewandowski, calling him "that boy from Znicz".

But Lewandowski shone from his very first moment at the club. The new forward scored a beautiful back-heel goal in his league debut against GKS Bełchatów, a 3-2 defeat, only four minutes after coming on as a substitute. With expectations raised, the press wanted the national team coach Leo Beenhakker to give the wunderkind his chance. "Is he a player who can fight with strong Czech Republic defenders who would want to kill him in every second of the match?" the Dutchman replied. He decided it was too early to call up the Lech player for Euro 2008. But a few weeks after the tournament it was time. After a draw at home to Slovenia, he picked Lewandowski for the next match, away at San Marino.

It was there, in the small Stadio Olimpico in Serravalle, that Lewandowski scored his first national team goal. He doesn't remember that either. Well, in all honesty neither does Poland, as the nation was stunned in the opening minutes when San Marino were awarded a penalty, only for Łukasz Fabiański to save from Andy Selva. Lewandowski came on in the second half and scored in the 68th minute, knocking in the rebound after an Ebi Smolarek shot to make it 2-0. Beenhakker used Lewandowski four

times during qualification for the 2010 World Cup, and he scored once more in Kielce, when Poland demolished San Marino 10-0. The team failed badly, finishing second-bottom in the six-team group, ahead only of San Marino. Beenhakker said this year how impressed he was with Lewandowski from the start, but there was no chance to use him the way he is being used by the current coach, Adam Nawałka. He was simply not the same player.

In fact, Lewandowski's record for the national team before the Euro 2016 qualifiers was far from impressive. Yes, he scored, but not against the biggest teams. He was often isolated because the 4-5-1 formation left him without support.

Lewandowski's time at Lech was almost perfect. They did well in Europe — for a Polish team — and won the Polish Cup in 2009. Lewandowski played a major role. Sharks started to swim around the Miejski Stadium in Poznań. Borussia Dortmund made their move. "They contacted me with an offer of around €2.5m," Kucharski said. By that time he had created a company helping players to develop – as he describes it – with the German co-owner Maik Barthel. His contacts in the German market were invaluable. The 21-year-old Lewandowski thought this could be his moment. But the club refused to let him go. The forward was devastated, although he now denies it. "I knew the next offer would come if only I played well enough," he said.

The facts are different: at the start of the season Robert had problems on the pitch. Some journalists began to suggest he was not focused enough. "It was only a moment. Few days. I'd be unhappy in his place," Kucharski said. "I'd feel the same if my transfer to Sporting Gijon in 1997 had been stopped by the club." The agent started to convince the young forward that it was only a matter of time. It worked. Ten months later Lewandowski, as Polish champion and Ekstraklasa top scorer, signed a deal with Dortmund worth €4.5m with an annual wage of €1m plus bonuses. "I remember he was so happy, but he knew from that moment he it was like starting over," said Iwona. "This was the chance his father wanted for him."

There were many offers, including one from Blackburn Rovers which was very attractive for Lewandowski. But he never had the chance to accept the invitation to fly there and negotiate because the Icelandic volcano Eyjafjallajökull stopped air traffic. "Dortmund were determined to sign me, I liked the club, the team and the coach seemed to be very interested, so everything looked optimistic," Lewandowski recalls.

He started to learn German. "It takes six months for him to speak fluently, so if we make another move to other country he will be ready very soon," Kucharski said with a big smile. But Lewandowski had his problems. Jürgen Klopp, the then Dortmund coach, tried him as number 10, with Lucas Barrios up front. Many experts in Poland thought that was the limit for Lewandowski.

"Barrios? Remember what I told you?" Kucharski laughs exactly the same way he did five years ago when I asked him about the Paraguay international. "Good, but not at Robert's level." It's important to have such confidence from your agent. Lewandowski needed a year to be played

as a number nine, but once Barrios had left, the Polish forward started to be the match winner. Dortmund impressed with the way they could transform themselves and started to counter and re-counter attack. Soon the theories about their success began. Why? How? "There were many, many details," Lewandowski explained. "For example, my wife, who is crazy about healthy food, helped me prepare for my challenges. I told the guys one day why I like different things to what everybody else was eating, so their wives started to call Ania. It's just one of hundreds of details. We changed our diets... Of course we worked very hard with the coach on every aspect of the game. Jürgen Klopp made me the footballer I am. I haven't changed anything at Bayern. I'm just using different weapons in my artillery, but I shaped my career in Dortmund."

Perhaps his mind was shaped even earlier, but his body was shaped at Dortmund. And the atmosphere was fantastic. I saw it myself, while speaking to Klopp in Marseille, after the final Champions League group game in December 2013. Lewandowski scored and his compatriots Jakub Błaszczykowski and Łukasz Piszczek both played as well. Klopp entered the area for TV rights holders, smiling as usual, and, seeing me talking to Błaszczykowski, started to swear in Polish. Błaszczykowski laughed. They high-fived and I could start my interview with the coach. "We've created a beast. You saw the beast? I did. It has your Polish name. Lewandowski. But tell the fans we are proud of everybody from your country..." Klopp started to flow immediately.

It was Lewandowski's final season at Dortmund. Two weeks later he confirmed he was moving to Bayern. It was a logical move, not changing country, language, the style of the opponent. When I heard about it, I simply couldn't believe it. Too good to be true? Nope. I remember it like it was today: 25 April 2010. Lech, fighting for the title, shared the points with their biggest rivals Wisła in Krakow. After the TV transmission I started my journey back to Warsaw. Not by train, as I came, but in a brand new Audi Q7, driven by Kucharski, whom I had known for years. Lewandowski's mother and sister were in the back seat, the first time I could witness the positive atmosphere in the family of Polish football's biggest star. We stopped at a small petrol station, about an hour outside Warsaw. "Tell me, what do you think Robert's future will be? Honestly?" I asked Cezary. "Bayern. After we finish the contract in Dortmund. We must prepare for the big jump," Kucharski replied. Iwona and Milena smiled; I thought Kucharski was just being nice to them.

When I talk to Kucharski now, he has the same confidence. "I wasn't lying that day," he said. "I really believed in Robert. I didn't know it would be Bayern, but for me they are among the top 10 clubs in the world, so moving to Munich was natural. And Robert knew he wasn't going to wear the yellow shirt for a lifetime. He never said anything like that, but we were honest with everybody there."

Is there a place for sincerity in football? Maybe the powers that be at Dortmund authorities should re-think this issue. One year before Lewandowski's contract expired Kucharski drove his next Audi Q7 — black this time — towards Dortmund. His player, scoring four against Real Madrid on the way to the Champions League final at Wembley, three years

less a day after our conversation about Bayern, proved himself again. "With bonuses Robert earned €1.5m," Kucharski explained. "I wanted him to get €5m, like Mario Götze did. But I heard that the maximum offer would be €3m. Why? You're not gonna believe this. 'Come on... This is a lot of money in Poland'. I left."

Kucharski stared his private conflict with the Dortmund authorities, but denies it lasted longer than Lewandowski's last day at the club. But it was certain his next move would be made within a few months. "I never thought about it," Lewandowski said. "This mess around me never gave me any extra pressure. I just did what I did." He raised his arms for a second. "What could I do? Nothing. My job was on the pitch and till the very last day I did my best for the team, the fans... We were lucky in Dortmund. I was one of the three best players there, we worked very hard and sometimes we were just lucky. That's it. Details."

Signing for Bayern made Lewandowski a very rich man. In 2013 Bayern offered €25m and were about to sign an €8m-per-year wage deal. But after selling Götze to Bayern, Dortmund made Lewandowski wait again. He signed the following summer, for free. He earns €11m a year with a big bonus at the start. His agent refuses to confirm it, but while talking to Polish *Playboy*, he admitted to having "earned 25 million euros during a supper" — which is presumably the bonus for contract signing. By then Jupp Heynckes, who had wanted Lewandowski, had been replaced by Pep Guardiola. The Catalan coach confirmed the transfer. Did Lewandowski hesitate? "Not even for a second. I know Pep had disliked some classical forwards in the past, but it didn't concern me. I wasn't there, I don't know much about these players. I know my quality. I knew I was ready and good enough. You know what the most interesting thing is about Pep? He likes to tell us, forward players, how much he trusts our instinct. People think sometimes that everything is programmed. It's not. In the defensive phase, Pep demands certain behaviour. But he tells us, 'Hey, I didn't play as a forward, so you tell me what you think and let's work on everything we need to.' I do what I feel is good for the team."

Asked about the main differences between Klopp and Guardiola, he is silent for a moment. "Hard to say... Maybe the warm-up? For Pep it's part of the game, he wants us to fight as hard as during the match. There aren't many differences I can speak about in public: both are top-class with great contact with the players."

How, then, was Lewandowski the number nine who survived under the high priest of tiki-taka? "I can speak only about myself. I'm versatile. I improve and feel I'm better with every month, but I'm not a classical centre forward. I'm good at attacking from the side, for example." He's not moved by statistics showing that his conversion rate is the best in Europe, far better than Lionel Messi or Cristiano Ronaldo. "They play in a different way and, besides, it doesn't matter how many times you take a shot. It only matters when you score."

Lewandowski's five goals in nine minutes against Wolfsburg, followed by some supreme performances for his country, have made him even more popular. He doesn't care. "He tells me, 'Mama, stop reading about me, it's pointless,'" Iwona says.

"Fame, fortune. It's part of my job, and I have to accept every positive and negative aspect of being professional footballer," said Lewandowski. I wondered if he ever steps out of his role, watching his answers.

"He's not acting," says Milena. "The problem with Robert is that you have to ask him exact questions or stop trying to know what he thinks. It's like he doesn't want to bother people with him. For me everything in his life makes perfect sense, the path he's walking, the choices he's made. Anna is very similar to our mother, very energetic, optimistic. I'm more like Dad, calm and quiet."

He never wanted his wedding to be sensational. Of course he couldn't avoid paparazzi, but it was as quiet as possible. There is a lot of crossover between the role he has to play and the reality. He doesn't follow his special diet, for instance, only because he has to. "I like it because it gives me the confidence that my body works in perfect condition," he explained when we met in Doha, Qatar, in January 2015. I'd gone for the handball World Championship; Robert was training and playing friendlies with Bayern. We sat in the lobby of the five-star Aspire Academy hotel, where the World Cup 2022 hosts house and train talented youngsters. The facilities are extremely impressive. I want to know how to lose a few pounds by changing my diet. "It's simple, there are rules," he said. "You start with something sweet, then you add another, then another in a certain order." He was at least engaged as when speaking about football.

Robert Lewandowski is a star. A predictable star – boring, some would say. But not for sponsors. Gillette, Panasonic, Nike, T-Mobile, Coca-Cola, Huawei. All the brands wanted to sign contracts in the local market, but it seems only a matter of time before he becomes a role model on the world stage. "I never had any problems with Robert," said Kucharski. "He perfectly understands that no scandal is good for his career. Well, there were some situations we had to handle, as with every human being, but we work so that nobody knew what we didn't want people to know." Observing Kucharski, I can't say whether he was joking or was serious. He surely means what he says, when he points out that Robert needs to become a marketing icon for a clothing company to be regarded as the world's best. Or one of the best.

Messi and Ronaldo have both found themselves criticised in their home countries for an inability to bring success in a national shirt. Trophies at club level only heighten the expectation of fans of the national team. With Franciszek Smuda as the national team coach, Lewandowski desperately wanted to achieve something on home soil in Euro 2012. In the first minutes of the opening match against Greece at the Stadion Naradowy in Warsaw, he starred. He scored a header and the country exploded with joy. But it all went wrong. Greece levelled and it finished 1-1. After another draw against Russia, Poland lost to the Czech Republic in Wrocław and finished bottom of the group. But the public didn't look for scapegoats. 100,000 people attended the Warsaw fan zone to thank the players for the efforts. Lewandowski, who wasn't the captain,

grabbed the mic: "I can promise you we will qualify for the next World Cup!" He made people scream the same way he did when he was scoring.

But it never happened. Under the new coach Waldemar Fornalik, Poland played without sparkle and Lewandowski had problems. In a 4-3-2-1 formation he had to fight against two or three opponents when receiving a pass. "I can run with the ball and I like running with the ball, but it's good to have many options to solve the situation," he said. The fans turned away and started to whistle their idol.

"The problem is that to qualify Poland will always need a goalscorer, and despite his huge quality Robert at that time was not the same player he is now," explained Andrzej Dawidziuk, one of national team's assistant coaches. "With him playing the way he plays now we would definitely have gone to Brazil. Obviously we would do other things differently as results say we made some mistakes, but it is true he is still becoming better and better."

Lewandowski became Poland's top club goalscorer in Europe, surpassing Włodzimierz Lubański's 31 goals for Górnik Zabrze and KSC Lokeren. Adam Nawałka, the former national team midfielder, was hired by new Polish federation (PZPN) chairman, the one-time Juventus and Roma star Zbigniew Boniek, and decided to give Lewandowski the support he needed. He gave him the armband and built the team around the Bayern forward. The effects were immediate. Lewandowski created the most effective partnership of the qualifiers with Ajax's young Arkadiusz Milik. After tough 2-1 win over Ireland at home, Poland could celebrate and

Lewandowski got the mic once again. "I believe in this team, I love these guys," he said. "But we know this is only a step. We haven't achieved anything yet. I can promise you we will our best in France!" His 13 goals in qualifying, equaling David Healy's record, were not the only reason to cheer him.

"I used to come here, where the Stadion Narodowy is. It's where my dreams started," Lewandowski said, recalling Communist Poland and the old Stadion Dziesięciolecia that stood on the same spot. Will Lewandowski be able to fulfil the dream this time? "I know him, and I know he will be prepared," said Iwona. "When I listened to him I closed my eyes. And I heard my husband. The same way of speaking, the same strong mentality." Words can't describe how proud she is.

So, what's the next move for the forward who now earns in ten minutes the monthly wage he received seven years ago at Znicz? The same wunderkind

from nearby Warsaw, who thanks to football is now co-owner of a successful venture capital fund? "I can tell you one thing." Kucharski decides to switch to mineral water. "And it's the first time I will. If Robert signs for Real Madrid... I don't say he will, but if — he would give this team more than Cristiano is giving them now. Not from the start, in his second season, when he settles. But he would." He speaks slowly, collecting his words. Kucharski still keeps the text message from José Mourinho, offering Lewandowski a contract while he was at Dortmund. "We had a gentlemen's agreement with Bayern. For me, that meant more than the better money offered in Madrid, so I thanked them and finished negotiations in Bavaria."

I tried to confirm this with Lewandowski. I called him late in the evening. "I like watching La Liga on TV," he said, "but I also like watching the Premier League. Nothing to say, I enjoy my time at Bayern. You know how agents are..." He laughs. So, nothing to say. Or maybe I just didn't ask the correct question.

88

Going To The Match

A Kickstarter project to create a visual celebration of football culture - http://bit.ly/blizz-gttm

By Przemek Niciejewski

104

Breeding Grounds

"You had to catch a bus to see the sun."

What's wrong with Finnish football?

As Iceland qualify for Euro 2016, Finland is asking, "Why not us?"

By Paul Brown

By the time the last cork had popped in Reykjavik, the inquest was well under way in Helsinki. Intrepid, tiny Iceland, with a population of just 329,000, blazed a trail for a string of minnow nations to follow by beating the odds and qualifying for Euro 2016. While this was rightly cause for celebration on a small island on the edge of the Arctic, it was also a source of embarrassment not far away in the coffee shops and saunas of one of its neighbours.

Finland, with a population of more than five million and a history of producing world class players like Jari Litmanen and Sami Hyypiä, will be looking on with envy as Lars Lagerbäck's men take on the best teams in Europe next summer. Because while Iceland has finally erupted on to the European stage like one of its many volcanoes, sleepy Finland, a land of deep forests, icy lakes and Father Christmas, remains in a deep freeze when it comes to football.

It is now the only Nordic country never to have qualified for a World Cup or European Championship.

The Finns are attempting to change that by taking a leaf out of Iceland's book and employing a Swede as coach. But while

Lagerbäck has worked wonders in his adopted country, what are the chances that Hans Backe, Sven Göran Eriksson's former assistant at Manchester City, can do likewise with his?

He doesn't have a lot to work with. The generation of Litmanen and Hyypiä is long gone and none of the current Finland team are household names. But even in their heyday the Finns never quite made it over the line. They last came close under Roy Hodgson in 2007, missing out in their final qualifier, a 0-0 draw with Portugal in Porto when a win would have taken them through.

So why the failure?

By another quirk of history, Finland is one of the only remaining European countries whose citizens are still required by law to do military service. This often takes young players away from their clubs at a crucial stage of their early development, sometimes for up to a year. Could it be holding back the nation's footballers?

In Finland, which shares a 1,000km border with a newly belligerent Russia, all men above the age of 18 are required by law to serve up to 347 days in the army. Refuse and you risk a prison sentence. This is not ideal if you are a promising young footballer. After all, you are unlikely to break into your first team or earn a move to a big European club if you're busy taking a year out learning how to fire a rifle in a forest.

And while the Finnish Defence Forces run a special programme for young athletes to combine their military service with sports training, this too can lead to problems. In the past, sportsmen have complained of exhaustion brought on by trying to combine army training with the demands of club football. Coaches have said they fear the system risks burning out players. In one case it even led to tragedy.

But the Finns are a proud people. They fought long and hard for their independence and military service is still regarded as an important act of patriotism which teaches you important life skills like leadership, teamwork and discipline. Could it really be holding them back on the football pitch?

Aki Riihilahti is 39. He is CEO of the biggest and most successful club in Finland, HJK, and has just been elected to the board of the European Clubs Association. In a 17-year career as a holding midfielder he played in five different countries, winning 69 caps for his country and scoring 11 goals, including one against England at Anfield.

Riihilahti, whose grandfather Yrjo fought in the snow against the invading Russian army in the Winter War of 1939-40, did his military service early on in his career, while he was injured. "I had a bad knee

injury so I was going to miss the whole football season anyway," he says. "I think you have to remember why we do it. Our grandparents fought for our independence and now to be a sovereign nation is still considered important.

"It gives you an understanding and respect for your own country and encourages teamwork and physical education. On the other hand, at an age when you should be concentrating on breaking through into the professional game, the amount of time spent in the service limits your time for training and recovery. Doing the service definitely helped me grow as a person, but if I had been fully fit I guess it would have been pretty difficult for me to get in the first team while I was doing it."

It didn't stop Hyypiä, although if anything he encountered the problem of training too much rather than too little. Now 41 and the manager of FC Zurich, Hyypiä was one of the most talented defenders of his generation. He played over 300 times for Liverpool and won 105 caps for Finland, succeeding Litmanen as captain.

He went into the army on his 19th birthday in 1992. At the time he was planning to look for a job in physical education and only decided on a career as a professional footballer while he was doing his term. Within the first month, he was allowed time out to train with the Dutch giants Ajax, who had just bought a rising star named Litmanen. Hyypiä also played his first full international while he was in the army.

But while his Finnish club MyPa thought they had arranged clearance for him and his teammate Toni Huttunen to be allowed leave from the garrison to train, things weren't quite that simple. In *Sami Hyypiä: From Voikkaa to the Premiership*, Hyypiä explains what happened on their first day, saying, "We went into the sergeant-major's office and asked if we could leave for training. Instead of the, 'Yes, everything is clear,' we expected, a raging sea of yelling was the only reply we got, as the sergeant-major let us know that you don't go anywhere on your first day in the army. Toni and I were in quite a panic." Eventually both players were allowed to train alongside their army duties, but Hyypiä admits the mental and physical strain of 11 months of constant travelling between garrison and club was tough.

Riihilahti, who is best known for his time in the Premier League with Crystal Palace, has seen just how tough first-hand. "Unfortunately ," he said, "we had one time in my regiment when an equestrian athlete was so tired he fell asleep while driving his car from camp to a horse-riding club where he was training. He survived. But there was a promising basketball player who died in similar circumstances."

In a bid to prevent such tragedies occurring again, the rules were changed to reduce the strain on athletes combining army life with training. "As far as I know it works pretty well now," Riihilahti went on. "From what I have heard athletes feel it is not preventing them doing their sport too much these days."

Army training can involve 6am runs around your barracks with a 66lb pack on your back, and live-firing and combat exercises "in terrain". But it's also about learning. "It's not really all about guns

and bullets like you'd see in military movies. It's more about education in a class room," Riihilahti said.

Sportsmen have also traditionally been afforded special treatment in Finland and allowed to serve a shorter term than the rest of the population. But a recent equality ruling by the Chancellor of Justice means this could change.

Martti Kuusela is 70. He is the most successful Finnish coach ever to have worked abroad, in a total of six different countries, winning championships in both his home nation and Hungary. As national team manager he missed out on qualification for the Mexico World Cup in 1986 by just two points.

At the time he also spent two days a week coaching an army team which contained many of the same players representing their country in qualifying, and was always aware of the physical and mental demands placed on them by combining army life with football. Looking back, Kuusela said, "When I was head coach in the 1980s I was also coaching the sport forces. When a player was in military service, we agreed to the load with the player and the army coaches.

"Too many young players have been spoiled by training too hard. But I always got information about what the player had done in the military. The military service time is strict time, but it is a good system for a player who wants to develop. I think in my coaching time the system was helping players – especially in other areas of life. They were able to improve individual properties, develop leadership skills and receive a good grounding for life in the future. Every nation needs its own armed forces and athletes and footballers want to meet their obligations."

Sportsmen are allowed to postpone their service. The tennis player Jarkko Nieminen took eight years to get around to it. In rare cases, some end up not doing it at all.

Shefki Kuqi, a barrel-chested bear of a man with huge hands and a laugh to shake a sauna, first came to Finland as an asylum-seeker from Kosovo before going on to play for the nation which took him in. A big, strapping striker, Kuqi went on to play for a host of English clubs, including Blackburn Rovers, Palace and Newcastle United, earning the nickname "Flying Finn" for his love of headed goals.

Although on paper he was perfect army material, he wasn't expecting his call-up papers until a change in the law meant naturalised citizens like him too were expected to take part. But after months of wrangling, he was allowed to swerve his tour of duty. "I got away with it because I've been living abroad," he said shortly after completing a switch to Blackburn in 2005.

Some expat Finns have taken other routes. Former Chelsea and Birmingham City striker Mikael Forssell did his military service in two stints well after he turned professional. Both times he did so during the close-season to limit the disruption to his career. Only Litmanen has scored more goals for Finland.

But national service cost Teemu Tainio a potential move to Manchester United

in 1997. The former Tottenham and Sunderland midfielder went for a trial at Old Trafford as a 16 year old and was invited back by Sir Alex Ferguson. "I played a few games, scored a few goals, and they wanted me to come back but I said: 'I have to do my army service'," Tainio revealed years later. He ended up moving to Auxerre instead and went on to become a mainstay of the Finland team.

Tainio said, "I spoke with Sir Alex and he said that he would love me to come back after my army service. But things change. I went to France and the rest is history. It was not a hardship for me because I actually enjoyed my time in the army.

"We also had an army football championship and I was voted Player of the Tournament! They knew I was an up-and-coming player and even allowed me to go out training before I returned to camp. The army also helped me become more disciplined and mature. It helped me grow up, and that helped me when I moved abroad."

Riihilahti agrees. "It has its good parts," he said. "It gives you a lesson in life. I grew from being a spoiled boy to a man. For many it's a question of honour and national identity to do it."

Sport and the military have long gone hand in hand in Finland. But football, though popular, has always been regarded as a secondary pastime. More than 150 promising athletes graduate every year from the Finnish Defence Forces Sports School, where half their service hours are dedicated to sports and related training.

But while its stated aims include producing two-to-four athletes capable of competing at the Olympics, the sports it focuses most on include rifle and pistol shooting, parachuting, track and field, orienteering and combat sports.

It could have been different. When the FDF first evolved out of the old White Guards who won the Finnish Civil War in 1918 after the country gained independence from Russia, football was one of the chief sports being pushed by the army to promote national pride and self-esteem.

But it lost out to *pesäpallo*, a Finnish version of baseball invented by Lauri "Tahko" Pihkala, an Olympic high jumper and discus thrower who was responsible for propaganda in one section of the White Guards. *Pesäpallo* went on to become Finland's national sport. Football never caught on in quite the same way and is still less popular than ice hockey and Formula One, despite more people playing it.

Finland has produced plenty of world champions in those sports, as well as others like rally driving, long-distance running, javelin and skiing. But it remains unable to break through in football. At the time of writing Finland are 64th in the world rankings, well below their peak position of 33, and there is little sign of that changing.

In a Euro 2016 group containing the Faroe Islands, Hungary, Greece, Romania and Northern Ireland, Finland managed to win just three matches out of ten and ended up fourth. Their last chance of qualifying disappeared in their penultimate game when the defensive midfielder Ovidiu Hoban scored an added-time equaliser for Romania against them, ending a goal drought that had stretched for so long it was a national record. It's difficult to think of a worse way to fail.

Reading the Mission Statement of the Finnish Defence Forces you see phrases like "troops must be able to endure combat with its various physical and mental challenges". Maybe Finns are just better fighters than they are footballers.

Kuusela is convinced military service helps the national team rather than hinders it. "In my opinion it's a good thing for the national team," he said. "We have been disappointed many times trying to qualify for major tournaments. We find many good explanations. But we're not good enough – yet."

Riihilahti is less certain about the army issue. But he sees more important factors at play. "We are too short-sighted in our approach," he said. "Firstly, the structure does not help as too many resources are lost in a conservative system which does not have a clear direction and lacks an understanding of the modern requirements of the game.

"We should first invest in facilities and youth development at clubs. Coaching and long-term plans for player development are a long road but it has to be started at all levels. At the moment it's too much about short-term survival and hoping that hiring the right national team coach changes everything

"I wouldn't like to say categorically that military service is a good or bad thing for the national team. But the best argument for doing it is that the best Finnish players like Litmanen and Hyypiä have all done it and it didn't stop them from becoming world class stars."

Where the next one will come from is the big question Finland's new coach must answer. Until he can, there is another phrase in that military handbook he should be mindful of. It reads, "Troops must be able to handle physical and psychological strain. Their leaders must prepare them for possible heavy losses"

Ⓑ

At the Feet of the Master

Gheorghe Hagi has established an academy to try to develop a new generation of Romanian talent

By Kit Gillet

On 23 May 2015, Gheorghe Hagi patrolled the edge of his technical area with studied rage, shouting words of heated encouragement and advice at his young players, led by their 21-year-old captain Bogdan Țîru. Viitorul Constanța, of which Hagi is both coach and owner, were 1-0 down against Brașov in their final home game of the Romanian Liga I season and needed a win to have any chance of qualifying for the following season's Europa League. The sun beat down as the clock ticked on.

The Viitorul players on the pitch were a youthful bunch. The average age of the squad was under 22 and most of the players had come through a football academy that Hagi, now 50, had set up in his hometown of Constanța in 2009, the same year the professional team he founded began its journey in Romania's third division.

Since then, the team has been promoted twice, so they play every week against the likes of Steaua and Dinamo, Bucharest clubs with proud traditions in global football. Meanwhile, the academy has grown to 300 players.

Among the players on the pitch against Brașov was Hagi's 16-year-old son Ianis, a diminutive but highly skilled No.10 who moved up from the academy late in the season. Some believe Hagi junior could eventually surpass his father as a footballer — no mean feat considering Hagi senior is the most famous player Romania has ever produced, a legend who wowed the world during the 1994 World Cup and who is one of the few players of any nationality to have turned out for both Barcelona and Real Madrid. By the time he retired at 36, Hagi had won domestic titles in Romania and Turkey, been named Romanian Footballer of the Year seven times and represented his country in three World Cups (1990, 1994 and 1998).

Like many of the Viitorul squad, Ianis wasn't alive to see his father's exploits during the 1994 World Cup and nor was he yet born when Hagi helped beat England 2-1 in the 1998 World Cup.

Hagi senior's reputation remains uncontested in his home country, and for more than six years he's been on a new mission: to revitalise Romanian football, putting his reputation, money and energy where his mouth is with his own football academy and professional team. Viitorul means 'future' in Romanian, while the academy is named after himself: the Gheorghe Hagi Academy.

Hagi's stated aim for both the academy and his professional team is simple:

to help develop new generations of gifted and tactically astute players who will not only dominate domestically but can return Romania to the highest international stage. "We have the talent, kids play football everywhere, every day, but we need to build a good environment to deliver for them," Hagi told me over coffee a few weeks before the game against Braşov. "Before I finished my playing career I had this idea to help young players fulfil their dreams, and I wanted to do this in the city where I was born."

In November 2013, when the Romanian national team crashed at the last hurdle, losing a play-off against Greece to fail to qualify for a World Cup for the fourth time in a row, no one in the crowded National Arena in Bucharest seemed surprised. "Romanian footballers suck," said a resigned fan standing next to me as the final whistle sounded, with a sad shake of his head. The stadium quickly emptied.

This was just the latest in a long string of disappointments for Romanian football fans and it wouldn't stop there.

In March 2014, the national hero and former Barcelona captain Gheorghe Popescu was sentenced to three years in prison for money laundering and tax evasion. His conviction kept him from being elected president of the Romanian Football Federation, a position he had been expected to take up. As part of the same case, seven other football executives and agents were also given jail terms.

Shortly after that, Dinamo Bucharest, one of Romania's leading teams, joined a long list of domestic teams that have filed for insolvency in recent years.

Steaua Bucharest had their own dramas: in December 2014 they had to play without their name or badge for several games – the scoreboard simply called them Home Team or Away Team – while they tried to negotiate an agreement with the Romanian army, which owns the Steaua name and badge and alleged that the team had been illegally using the brand since 2004. Holding up the negotiations may have been the fact that Gigi Becali, the larger-than-life owner of Steaua, had been sentenced to three years in prison in May 2013 for his role in illegal land transactions. He was released early in March 2015. Steaua now have a new badge but reached an accord with the Ministry of Defence to continue to use the Steaua name.

In among all of this, Hagi seemed to be one of the few untainted and bona-fide football heroes Romania had left. "Why did I choose to join the academy and play for Viitorul? Simple: Hagi," Ţiru told me the day before their final home game of the season.

Outside the small city of Ovidiu, on the Romanian coast just north of the port city of Constanţa, the Gheorghe Hagi Football Academy stands among a series of sloping fields. A gravel driveway leads up to the complex and the small stadium that Viitorul Constanţa will occupy from next season. (The first team currently play their home games in an old stadium on the outskirts of Bucharest, since their own stadium, with 4,500 seats, wasn't ready for top-division football.)

Despite it being almost summer a cold wind whips up from the Black Sea, visible a few kilometres away. Behind the main stadium, academy players from the Under-13, Under-15, Under-17 and Under-19 teams run through practice drills on two of the four standard-sized pitches, watched over by coaches who are using the same sets of drills and tactics for each age group, following the example of clubs such as Ajax. The older age groups have heart monitors recording their exertions during training, so that coaches know who is not working hard enough or if the drills are not having the desired effect.

Further back is the skeleton of a large building which when finished will house staff offices and accommodation for the older academy players, 60 of whom are currently living in a hotel the academy has rented 20 minutes drive from the complex. From the unfinished building's fourth floor you can look down on the entire facility, seen by many as among the best in the country. By some estimations, Hagi and his backers have spent €10million on the infrastructure.

Workmen are still busy on the complex's main stadium, trying to get it ready in time for the 2015-16 season, so that the first team can finally return to their home and start developing proper links to the city and their potential fan base – at the "home" game against FC Braşov barely 500 people had shown up, highlighting both the newness of the team and also the general mood surrounding Romanian football at the moment. Turnstiles were added at the entrance to the stadium just a few days before my visit, but the fence is yet to go up so you can just walk around them. (In one of those only-in-Romania situations, Steaua boss Gigi

Becali was granted day release from prison in April 2014 to perform unskilled labour at the academy, although the likelihood that he actually mowed any grass or painted any fences is minimal.)

After a string of short managerial stints in Turkey and Romania in the early 2000s, Hagi returned to Constanţa and, at a time when there were few grassroots organisations operating in the country, set up the academy, which is now one of the main suppliers of players to the national youth teams. The national U17 team recently had nine players from the academy in its squad, while the U15 and U19 regularly have five or six academy players.

In May 2014, Viitorul player Cristian Manea became at 16 the youngest Romanian to play for the national team and in the same game the club's 19-year-old midfielder Florin Tănase also made his international debut. Romania beat Albania 1-0. "We invest in the young, promote the young, we put 17 year olds, 19 year olds in the first team, we give them a chance," said Hagi, adding that by 2020 he hopes "we can have 11 [academy] players in the [senior] national team."

The Hagi Academy has attempted to offer something that has been lacking elsewhere in Romanian football for some time: a holistic approach. "You have to look to youth, but you can't just take the youth and put them on a field with a ball. This is not football, it's a kickabout," said Lucian Burchel, the academy's technical director, who first played with Hagi when they were 13 year olds and later spent five years working for the Romanian Football Federation before joining Hagi's project in its infancy.

The great Romania national teams from the 1980s and 90s were raised in this holistic way because of the communist system in place before 1990. Youth players were housed together and spent most of their waking lives together, which helped create bonds and understanding between players. "They took care of everything, we came to Bucharest, lived together for three or four years. From that came the team of the 1990s," said Hagi.

The Gheorghe Hagi Academy now has more than 300 players from across Romania and many of the older kids live away from home, under the care of the academy. "We have to be very responsible for the players, taking them from their families," said Burchel. However, he believes the holistic approach, which is prevalent in countries such as Spain and Germany, is beneficial. "If you have the routine of going to school together, resting together, playing together, it helps. In the hotel each group has a program – school program, training program, rest program."

The players even have Spanish language classes, and, from next season, English, to increase their chances of and comfort in playing abroad at a later point in their careers. "In Romania, until Hagi came here with the academy, Romania didn't invest much in young players," Nicolae Roşca, the U17 coach told me, sitting in a hotel's noisy canteen surrounded by players grabbing their lunch before a relaxation period and then afternoon training. Roşca, a central defender who retired a decade ago, has been working at the academy since 2009, moving from

coaching roles with the U10 and U19 teams to his present position. "It's all about the money," he said. "It's hard to invest in young players because you don't know if you are going to get anything back."

The U17 team had just returned from Italy, where they played (and won) two friendlies against AC Roma's U17 team. "Italy was tough, we had to play very well," said Mihai Ene, a 16 year old who plays in midfield for the academy's U17 team. Dressed in flowery shorts and a bright yellow T-shirt, his hair in a quiff, Ene understands English but feels more confident replying to my questions in Romanian. He's been at the academy for three years, but originally comes from the industrial city of Ploieşti. "Here we are trained tactically, technically and mentally. Where I came from before it was just fun really," he said. "At the beginning it was very hard to leave my family, but they come here often and I go home regularly."

Photos from academy games decorate the lobby walls around us, while a handful of players visit the small clinic on the ground floor. Timetables pinned to the wall list study and training plans, while another shows the television schedule for the Champions League final and upcoming Viitorul games. The place needs a lick of paint, as would anywhere that has 60-plus teenage boys living in it.

Over the last few years the academy's youth teams have dominated domestically. The U13, U15, U17 and U19 squads won six of a possible twelve national championships between the 2011-12 and 2013-14 seasons, and made a clean sweep of it in the 2014-15 season (with the U19 top by 19 points and the U13 team scoring almost twice as many goals as all but the runners up – and that was the Academy's U13 B team). In November 2014, its U12 team represented Romania at the Danone Nations Cup in Brazil, finishing sixth and beating the representative teams from Germany, Algeria and Italy.

All of this has required significant investment and Burchel says that the reason other teams in Romania aren't doing this is that they are too focused on short-term needs and aren't willing to invest in developing players. "Steaua doesn't have an academy. Why? Because after four or five years the owner asks: 'Where is the player from my academy in the first team? Show me.' And the manager says we don't have one. 'Where is the player from the academy we sold for money?' 'We don't have one'," he says, with a shrug of his shoulders."

However, there are concerns about the long-term financial sustainability of Hagi's project as well as the ability of such a youthful first team squad to compete at the very top. The hope is that the academy will become self-sufficient in five or six years, selling players to other teams in Romania and abroad and using the money to fund the academy's operations. So far, however, the money has mostly come from Hagi and his business partners.

And, after only just surviving relegation in the 2013-14 season, Hagi brought in several veterans to the first team to help guide the younger players. "The young players in our first team don't have everything yet," admits Burchel. "Bringing in players like Bănel Nicoliță [who played for Steaua between 2005-11 and then in

France for Saint-Étienne and Nantes] helps. He is someone who can take our players and push them, help them develop by example. Nicoliță took our captain after training and helped him develop."

The 21-year-old Țîru agrees. "I became captain this year," he told me. "The first games were a bit hard but now it's okay. I know what being a captain means."

Before the Brașov game, Viitorul Constanța were in ninth place in the table, but with some of the teams above them in insolvency they had a chance of qualifying for the Europa League if they won both remaining games and other results went in their favour. "Playing in Europe would be big step," said Țîru, sitting in the team's hotel on the outskirts of Bucharest. "It would be a reward for the job we've been doing the last few years. Two games, six points. We will see."

The larger challenge remaining, however, is finding room for all of the academy players maturing from the youth set up. Viitorul currently have a B team that will play in the Romanian third division in 2015-16, but there are obviously only a limited number of positions available in either squad: many players will not make it and will struggle to find another team.

Hagi is hopeful that as the academy's reputation grows further, more of the young players will find a future at other clubs throughout the leagues. He is also optimistic that their best players will eventually end up plying their trade across the world. "We are open to selling players," he said. "Our target is to build a competitive player and then, our level is our level, so if they can be more than us they can move on."

In June it was reported that Chelsea have agreed a deal to sign Cristian Manea from Viitorul for £2.3million, with the right-back likely to spend a season at Chelsea's associate club, Vitesse Arnhem. In December 2012 the club sold the striker Gabriel Iancu to Steaua for an undisclosed fee. Steaua subsequently put a €25 million buyout clause in his contract.

"We are not England, Germany, Spain," said Hagi. 'We don't have money to buy the best players so we have to build them. Then we can one day compete with the others who have money, full stadiums every week. One day we beat them, that is my target. That level of respect."

As the final minutes tick down against Braşov, Viitorul Constanţa have much of the possession, but it is clear that they will be unable to pull back a two-goal deficit. "Maybe they are tired or maybe it is because they are young," one employee tells me after the game ends 2-0. "They don't have the experience yet of dealing with the end of the season."

Despite this, many in Romania hope Hagi and his young players are ones to watch in the years to come. Indeed, a few weeks after finishing eleventh, it was announced that Ianis Hagi was joining Serie A side Fiorentina, for a fee of around €1 million.

The Hagi legacy continues.

Slaggy Island

South Bank was a grim industrial pocket of Teesside – and the home to a wealth of footballing talent

By Harry Pearson

When former Northern Ireland and Middlesbrough winger Terry Cochrane signed for South Bank in 1992 the Teesside non-League club had problems. Thieves got in the ground at night, lifted tools from the shed, forced entry to the club house, fled with booze. The Bankers took measures. They bought a powerful Rottweiler. When training ended for the day, they let him loose and locked the gates. That night thieves broke in again, stole the dog.

"That's South Bank," Terry Cochrane said, "fella has two ears they think he's a cissy."

South Bank lies three miles east of Middlesbrough. Locally they call it Slaggy Island in honour of the ring of spoil heaps that once cut it off from the outside world. It's not as glamorous as that nickname makes it sound. South Bank was the home of the Smith's Dock shipyard, of Bolckow Vaughan and Dorman Long steelworks, clusters of iron foundries, warrens of brickyards. Blast furnaces, smelters, rolling mills and fabrication sheds converted ore to pig iron, iron to steel. They shaped it, cut it and shipped it out. Through most of the 20th century Slaggy Islanders lived their lives under a cloud of bitter smog. You had to catch a bus to see the sun.

Yet there was a power and a magic to it. The sparks off arc welders and angle-grinders danced in the darkness and at night the sky was dyed a dirty orange and pulsed like a heart. When South Bank's most celebrated son, Wilf Mannion – Tom Finney said the forward played the game like an angel – called his hometown "the enchanted city" he wasn't being ironic.

South Bank FC was founded in 1868, the first football club in the north east of England. The Ellis Cup was launched – as the South Bank Amateur Challenge Cup – in 1889, which makes it either the fourth or fifth oldest football competition on the planet (the Northern League – of which South Bank was a founder member – began the same year).

Originally for under-18 teams, the Ellis Cup soon expanded to include senior sides too, not just from South Bank but from across Teesside and down into the mining villages of the North York Moors and Cleveland Hills. Over the following century more than 100 players who would turn pro played in it, among them some of the most influential figures in the English game.

George Elliott, my grandfather's boyhood hero, played in the Ellis Cup for Redcar Crusaders, signed for South Bank shortly afterwards, then for Middlesbrough. Aided by two other Ellis Cup Slaggy Islanders, the Carr brothers, Jackie and Willie, Elliott hit 31 goals in 32 league matches in 1913-14, helping Boro to third place in the English top flight, their highest ever finish.

George Hardwick's father worked in the ironstone mines of East Cleveland. Hillbilly country. My aunties lived up there, in a village of half a dozen terraced streets surrounded by the purple moor tops. Shooed outside to play, I'd take my Ayresome Angel football out into the back alley, come scuttling back two minutes later. Even in the 1960s the local kids threw stones at strangers.

Hardwick senior's mine shut down. Money was so short it could crawl under a duck. The Hardwicks went out at dawn, collected mushrooms to make a meal. Hardwick's mother picked up old jumpers, unravelled them and knitted George a red jersey and matching socks to play his football in. He turned out in the Ellis Cup for Saltburn, moved on to South Bank, signed for Middlesbrough in 1937. A cultured full-back, Hardwick had a matinee idol moustache and the face and physique to match. When he smiled, women's legs turned to jelly. My granddad called him 'Gorgeous George' and blew sarky kisses to him from the Ayresome Park chicken run. Hardwick laughed off the abuse. He captained club and country, people whispered happily of an affair with a Hollywood 'It Girl': Ava Gardner, Rita Hayworth, accounts varied.

The Golden Boy, Wilf Mannion, was born in Napier Street, South Bank. The blast furnaces spewed and roared a hundred yards from his front door. He grew up too poor to afford a football. "We used to get a pig's bladder from the butchers, blow it up," he told me once. "Played on a pitch of cinders. I tell you what, anyone can control a pig's bladder is a ruddy genius."

Mannion won the Ellis Cup with South Bank St Peter's when he was 16. His side played South Bank East End in the final. East End's stopper got no closer to the blond inside-forward than kicking the ball into his groin. The stopper's name was Harold Shepherdson. Three decades later, as Alf Ramsey's assistant, he'd be leaping off the bench at Wembley when Geoff Hurst scored England's fourth, the manager barking, 'Sit down, Harold, I can't see,' at his back.

Wilf joined Hardwick in a Boro team that included other Ellis Cup alumni. Micky Fenton from South Bank East End was the centre-forward, quick as mercury, powerful in the air, with a shot that thumped off his boot with a thud like Joe Louis hooking the heavy bag. Bobby Stuart, the right-back, another South Banker, won two caps with England in 1936 and was chosen by Wills Tobacco as the Boro player for that year's cigarette card set, alongside Raich Carter, Ted Drake and a youthful, grinning Stanley Matthews.

With George, Wilf, Micky and Bobby, Boro finished seventh in 1937, fifth in 1938 and fourth in 1939. If it hadn't been for the war we'd have won the title, George Hardwick said. Bloody Hitler.

The influence of Slaggy Island's football trophy spread far beyond Teesside. The future Leeds United capo, Don Revie, played in the Ellis Cup for Middlesbrough

Swifts. The Manchester United boss, Matt Busby, a serviceman at Catterick Garrison, helped Portrack Shamrocks defeat Cargo Fleet Home Guard in the 1946 final. Ken Furphy turned out for Stockton West End, went pro with Everton, achieved great things coaching Watford and ended up in the USA in the 1970s managing New York Cosmos, pairing Pelé with Giorgio Chinaglia up front.

Bobby Smith worked down the ironstone mine in Hardwick's home village of Lingdale, hewing rock in drift seams 200 feet below the heather. At 15 he hit a hat-trick for Redcar Albion in the Ellis Cup, at 16 he was signed by Chelsea. When he left Stamford Bridge for Spurs in 1955 he asked if he could keep his number nine shirt as a souvenir. Chelsea told him he couldn't. Shirts were expensive and they didn't have enough.

Smith had the big, rugged face of the northern working man, pickaxe-wielders' arms, a tugboat torso. He was the man in the pub whose drinking arm you'd least want to jog. Spurs' captain Danny Blanchflower spoke of glory, of playing the game "the right way". Up front his centre-forward banged in goals and terrorised opponents, literally. Preparing for corners, defenders would look up to see Smith pointing at them, bellowing, "You're going to fucking get it." In the 1963 Cup-Winners' Cup final against Atlético Madrid, the ex-miner took care of his marker early, decking him with an elbow to the slats. Spurs won 5-1. Bobby Smith was 5'9", but he seemed far bigger.

My friend's dad was the goalkeeper for the village team. Years later he'd recall an Ellis Cup match against Great Broughton — managed in those days by the village postmistress Nancy Goldsborough — when a shiny-eyed teenage centre-forward banged in a hat-trick and at the final whistle wandered over, patted my friend's dad on the arm, told him. "One day, when I'm playing for England, you'll brag to your mates about this," he smiled and introduced himself: "I'm Brian Clough."

"If he hadn't been so little, I'd have planted him," my friend's dad said, telling the story for the thousandth time.

From the late seventies onwards hardship battered Teesside. The steelworks and the shipyards shut. The population of South Bank dwindled. Shutters went up over doors and windows, shops closed, derelict streets were bulldozed. Football clung on. Barely.

After Terry Cochrane quit, South Bank's ground was attacked routinely and severely. Vandals smashed the windows. Arsonists burned down the clubhouse, torched the main stand. Somebody took a sledgehammer to the dugouts, carted off the bricks. By the late 1990s the pitch was three feet deep in grass, a stadium that had once held 8,000 for cup ties looked like a bomb site. Unable to fulfil fixtures, the Bankers had long since been suspended from the Northern League they'd co-founded.

Now there's a community centre, named Golden Boy Green in honour of Wilf Mannion, where the ground once stood. There's a skateboard park and a basketball court, no football, no memorial. These days South Bank FC play at Harcourt Road, sharing the pitch with Eston Villa and Middlesbrough Homeless. They're in the Stockton Sunday League. In 2015 they got to the final of the Ellis Cup, won it in a penalty shoot-out against North Ormesby Cons.

The Ellis Cup is 126 years old. The elaborate silver trophy still resides on Slaggy island, in Normanby Road just up from Golden Boy Green. It's on display in the Erimus Social Club. Visitors are welcome. A full set of ears is still not mandatory, though a romantic attachment to the past will come in handy.

B

121

Theory

"Everyone in an organisation keeps on getting promoted until they reach their level of incompetence."

The Peter Principle

Promotion to a level of incompetence is a common idea in business, but is it true in football?

By Rupert Fryer

Player recruitment is at an all-time high. Swelling squads built to combat the increasing physical demands of the game in a fully globalised industry are creating an increasing number vacancies at every level of the food chain, leaving the game's employees rushing though doors that are revolving at increasingly dizzying speeds. The latest Fifa TMS Global Transfer Market report says the game's governing body handled 13,090 international transfers in 2014, totalling US$4.06 billion — an increase of 2.9% on 2013.

One good season is now usually enough to earn a big move, with the contemporary world of professional football dictating that any player who excels for a club outside Europe's elite is instantly rewarded with step up to bigger things. But beware, bigger does not always mean better and football's current landscape is claiming more and more victims of the game's Peter Principle — a business theory particularly applicable to the plight of the workers navigating this brave new world.

First posed by Dr Laurence J Peter and Raymond Hull in their 1969 book *The Peter Principle*, Andrea Ovans in the *Harvard Business Review* labelled the work a "wicked satire", explaining

its fundamental conceit as follows: "Everyone in an organisation keeps on getting promoted until they reach their level of incompetence. At that point they stop being promoted."

Promotion in the football world time and again transforms talented and ambitious young athletes into incompetents, reducing them to another on the long list of Peters. From Shaun Wright-Phillips, Stewart Downing and Andy Carroll to Felipe Melo, Ishak Belfodil and Juan Iturbe, we're left with constant reminders that a medium-sized fish may well star in small ponds but can struggle when plunged into deeper waters.

After the teenage prodigy Iturbe made a stuttering start to his career, failing to break through at FC Porto, a single season impressing for Verona in 2013-14 convinced Roma to splash out around €25 million for his services. At Verona things had clicked for Iturbe. Be it the environment, emotional tone, tactical set-up or a combination of all three, the Argentinian found the conditions in which he could thrive. But come the summer of 2015, Iturbe is just another Peter, bearing a closer resemblance to the player who struggled to perform in the depressingly weltering standard of Argentinian football during a loan spell with River Plate in 2013.

Still just 22 years old, he may well come good for Roma, but with the immediacy of the modern game, coupled with the fact that Roma are hardly in a position to invest that sort of money on speculative punts for the future, the club would have hoped for more. Similarly, Wright-Phillips and Downing starred for relatively humble sides before being promoted to levels of incompetence, with Chelsea and Liverpool respectively. Both saw their careers quickly peter out once they were asked to strut a grander stage.

Failing to make an impact when that big transfer arrives inevitably leads to accusations of a lack of desire, application, and/or talent. But for many of football's Peters, it's too simplistic to attribute a solely personal responsibility for their misadventures.

With more talented individuals around them to alleviate the burden, it's unfair to expect a player to have the same sort of impact they did further down the employment ladder, as the skillset required to perform in humbler surroundings isn't necessarily transferable. In the same way a lead salesman may have the gift of the gab at your local call centre but be entirely unsuited to the position of team leader, performing at one club can require a markedly different set of attributes from those required to do so at a higher level. The danger, as Rob Asghar said of the Peter Principle in his 2014 piece for *Forbes Magazine*, "Incompetence Rains, Er, Reigns: What The Peter Principle Means Today", is that "When you're great at something, you might get rewarded with a promotion ... into something you're terrible at."

There are countless examples. The Brazil international Felipe Melo could get on with destroying at Fiorentina, but at Juventus he was required to play football, too; the result of his €25 million switch to Turin was desperately predictable. Clint Dempsey could concentrate on charging into the penalty area, often ignoring teammates and smashing speculative shots at goal for Fulham, but his talents weren't compatible with a more holistic attacking approach he found among an increased number of talented individuals at Tottenham Hotspur. Ashley Young was forgiven for risking possession as he sought to be the difference-maker for Aston Villa, but he struggled with the more intricate play demanded of him at Manchester United, who dominated games more regularly, leaving his technical limitations exposed at the very top. "Subsequent discussions [of the Peter Principle]," says Ovans, "begin to recognise that problematic bosses aren't so much utterly incompetent as so good at something that their failings are overlooked."

Some are able to escape the dangers of becoming just another Peter, however, be it by hook or crook. Marouane Fellaini appeared set to become 2013-2014's highest profile Peter following his move from Everton to Manchester United – a transfer, incidentally, brought about due to the managerial Petering of David Moyes. Fellaini's physical, battering ram-like attributes fit the collective functioning of Moyes's Everton side which sought to exert its physical dominance, maximise set pieces and gain territory by playing vertical passes. At Old Trafford, his technical deficiencies were brutally exposed.

Thankfully for the Belgian, the Peter previously in charge of his fortunes was replaced by the more competent Louis van Gaal, whose eternal desire to innovate forced a solution, in this instance by utilising Fellaini as a deep-lying target man, as Jonathan Wilson noted in the *Guardian*: "If Fellaini looks out of place – as though the real footballer has escaped and his fellow POWs are trying to con the guards that he's still in the line at roll-call with a model constructed from the contents of the broom cupboard – it's because he is out of place, and that is what makes him devastating."

Fellaini clearly doesn't have the same impact on his new team as he did on his old, but his level of Petering has been reduced, as was James Milner's following his £26 million switch from Aston Villa to Manchester City in 2010. Perhaps Milner had read HBR's *Making Yourself Indispensable*, which Ovans describes as offering up "a step-by-step guide to making the most of your strengths, so that your weaknesses don't matter". After quickly accepting he would not be able to star as a flying winger or creative attacking midfielder at club that had invested hundreds of millions in an attempt to assemble a squad capable of doing battle with Barcelona and Real Madrid, Milner reinvented himself as an industrious employee who was willing to forgo the fanfare of his previous position and accept a less recognised, but equally important, admin role. Downing, meanwhile, was able to address his decline by utilising an escape route less prevalent in the business world – dropping back down to a more natural level at West Ham.

The risk of Petering is one of football's few true constants, because as the game's clubs scramble to ascend to greater heights at every opportunity so do its workers. A player's desire to improve his life away from a game that is now producing millionaires on a scale never before seen in professional sports understandably adds to the incentive of chasing that big promotion. As in any industry, workers follow the money. In a refreshingly candid moment following his much-criticised switch from Atlético Mineiro in Brazil to China's Shandong Luneng in January 2015, then first-choice Brazil striker Diego Tardelli said, "A wage rise is part of an athlete's life, of everyone's who has to go to work." Coupled with the competitiveness essential to any top-level sportsman, we're inevitably left the overwhelming majority of players striving to test themselves at the highest possible level.

But the result for the game as a whole, as Rory Smith noted in "The Death of Mystery" in *The Blizzard* Issue Ten, has seen the dominant elite now living by the mantra "if you can't beat them, take them." The elite are stockpiling the talent, leaving the chasing pack further and further behind. As Curtis Jackson once posed, "the rich get richer, and the poor don't get a fucking thing." The last 11 Champions League titles have been won by teams from the game's four richest leagues: England, Spain, Italy and Germany. All 20 semi-finalists from the last five editions came from those same nations.

Football is a business like any other, but with one major exception: success is not noted on balance sheets but judged by the content of the trophy cabinet. Lifting the titles to fill those cabinets, however, is now more dependent than ever before on those balance sheets, and the recruitment and upkeep of workers who command such high salaries remains the game's biggest expenditure. Analytics experts tell us that success is largely dependent on wages spent: the Football Benchmark database launched by the sports team at the professional services firm KPMG found that every Champions League winner since 2011-12 had staff costs in excess of €200 million.

And we're now at a stage where, for those lucky few, even the creation of Peters isn't much of a problem. While in the business world a large number of Peters are born in-house, football requires its workers to relocate, leaving a knock-on effect that can result in ostensibly ill-conceived promotions proving successful.

The Germany international Mario Götze has, thus far, failed to reproduce for Bayern Munich the stunning displays that made him one of the hottest properties in European football prior to his arrival from Borussia Dortmund. However, he is one of many Peters who has strengthened his current workforce by weakening the competition. For Bayern in 2013, making Dortmund weaker was just as important as making themselves stronger. The rest of the top clubs in the Bundesliga seem to take it in turns to challenge Bayern's dominance and the club have reacted by persistently cherry-picking the best from any would-be pretender to their crown. Anyone displaying the gall to step into their arena is quickly slapped down. Bayer Leverkusen's challenge at the turn of the millennium, for example, was quickly scuppered as Bayern pinched Michael Ballack, Zé Roberto and later Lúcio. 27

of Bayern's 50 most expensive signings arrived from Bundesliga rivals.

Professional football is widely regarded to be at the highest level the sport has ever seen, particularly the latter stages of the Champions League, with the riches on offer attracting the world's elite athletes. But without all the stockpiling, with fewer Peters, one wonders if the greatest show on earth could be even greater. Had the likes of Scott Sinclair continued darting in from the channels for Swansea instead of warming the bench at Manchester City, had Belfodil continued bullying Serie A's best defenders for Parma instead of kicking his heels on Inter's training ground, the overall standard of the game would be even better.

From a footballing point of view, continuing to star at a lower level rather than accepting a promotion which results in a more marginalised role would be of more benefit to the game as a whole. Matthew Le Tissier amassed a stunning highlights reel over a career at Southampton that one struggles to see him replicate in a team of higher quality which would undoubtedly have demanded a greater contribution to the collective. Juan Román Riquelme, likewise, could only exist in a team in which the entire functionality of the play depended solely on his individual freedom, and so accepted his time would be best spent back at Boca Juniors. Antonio Di Natale has been a phenomenon for the less-fancied Udinese, while Rogério Ceni has carved out his own special legacy in Brazil by electing to remain at São Paulo for his entire career. Hakan Şükür lost two years failing to make the grade at Inter, Parma and Blackburn Rovers before resuming his remarkable career in his rightful home of Istanbul, scoring almost 300 goals for Galatasaray and winning eight league titles and a Uefa Cup.

But most take the bait and accept the risk of joining the game's list of Peters. And so the 2015-16 season sees the likes of Manchester City's Fabian Delph, Napoli's Mirko Valdifiori, Roma's Iago Falque, Tottenham's Toby Alderweireld and Kieran Trippier, Atlético Madrid's Luciano Vietto, Liverpool's Christian Benteke and Danny Ings and Juventus's Paulo Dybala all striving not to see themselves heading for the Petering trajectory of Dejan Lovren, Jack Rodwell, Geovanni, Miralem Sulejmani or Asier Illarramendi.

The list of football's Peters will continue to grow. To the detriment of everyone save a few bank managers and, as always, a few of the game's elite. ⒷⒷ

Chaos Theory

With so many variables at play, does anybody ever know anything?

By Alex Keble

In football, narrative is everything; from intricate statistical analysis to romanticised headlines, the concept of linear progression – completed stories with beginnings and ends, with heroes and villains – fuels our obsession. Every season is the next novel, with new plot lines and twists, and every match is the next set-piece, anticipated and adored for its function in the narrative arc.

Where art ricochets through the crisis of post-modernism, sport continues to offer us the comforting illusion of linearity and progression, a cause-and-effect safety net. And as spectators and humans, we crave the world that we create; it is a world in which all variables can be harnessed and understood, where ascent and decline can be analysed and accounted for, and where coaches and players control their own destiny. We may at times enjoy the "unpredictability", but for the most part, sport conforms to a deeply instinctive human yearning for a version of reality that, after 200 years of existential angst in art and philosophy, is consistently denied: concrete meaning and the rejection of chaos.

In truth, the deeper we dig in our analysis of the game, the more this simplified model of causality is called into question. Is it time to re-think the way in which we structure commentary and analysis,

and in doing so, radically re-evaluate our understanding of football?

All football commentary, from the *Sun* to *The Blizzard*, works on the basis that football is, to some extent, predictable and explainable; the signings, tactics, and performances are constantly analysed, in order to project future outcomes or justify results. The quality of the journalism may change the extent to which this idea is believed (many do recognise the complexity of variables and the chaos of sporting outcome), but nevertheless most of us believe, to some extent, that in-depth tactical analysis can tell us how and why a given result was reached.

However, this idea is difficult to accept when we consider the impact of chaos theory.

In a close match entering extra time at 0-0, we can accept that a number of minor incidents could have changed the name on the World Cup trophy. The BBC's commentary team focused on Martin Demichelis being caught between tracking Thomas Müller and dropping onto Mario Götze for that vital goal. Others focused on Ezequiel Garay's slowness to cover, Jogi Löw's substitutions or Rodrigo Palacio's miscontrol when clean through on goal moments before. But the truth is, all of these things affected the outcome, as did every other moment in this match, every other moment in the World Cup and every other moment in the history of world football.

Like a sentient chessboard, football – as a humanly contained space of fixed boundaries and variables – perfectly displays the frightening reality of chaos theory. Chaos theory describes a world of non-linear dynamics, in which each microscopic element of reality is chaotically entangled with its surroundings. The archetypal example – a butterfly flapping its wings in Brazil causing a tornado in Texas – may help illuminate the idea of chain reactions, but to conceptualise chaos theory fully we must realise that the web of interconnectivity is virtually infinite; as a microcosm of reality, football cannot escape the clutches of determinism.

On a pitch, every movement of the ball affects the positioning of multiple players. The match shifts with every touch and therefore the potential pathways for the future also shift, irreversibly. If player A passes the ball 10 yards to his or her left, players all over the pitch will move to accommodate the play. Even if the ball is instantly switched back to player A, countless variables have changed with the passage of time – from runs made to weather conditions — and all future action in the match has been affected by that initial decision. If we accept that the positioning of any single player on the pitch affects the passing and movement options of the player on the ball, it is self-evident that the number of variables affecting the next millisecond of a match are uncountable. Each decision creates a ripple effect of

variables, expanding into a Cantorian infinity of responses, and responses to responses, until it becomes clear that the events of a football match can unfold in an infinite number of ways and that every minuscule action has a dramatic, irreversible effect on this outcome.

In simpler terms, if André Schürrle had turned back and passed the ball inside to Müller, rather than crossing for Götze in that decisive moment in the 118th minute, the action would have been affected and countless players would have repositioned themselves (not least the two 'caught out' Argentina centre-backs). Müller could have been tackled and Argentina could have broken away to score the winning goal, or he could have reworked the attack so that it was still Philipp Lahm lifting the trophy. This part is easy to accept.

But in truth, there are thousands of different touches and movements Schürrle could have made, each affecting the potential decisions of other players on and off the ball, over the five seconds that followed. The chain reaction of decision-making continues to inflate exponentially over the following two minutes: considering that each decision will shift the match slightly, it quickly becomes evident that there are tens of trillions of potential outcomes to this football match. In any given game, each microscopic movement or decision – anywhere on the pitch – permanently denies trillions of potential pathways, whilst simultaneously opening up trillions of new ones.

We tend to trace the route of a goal back to the opening of the move – or at most, the breakdown of the previous one

– when in truth its foundations stretch back to kick-off and the first decisions made by every player on the pitch. The reason Götze scored that goal was no more because of Schürrle's trickery or Götze's skill, as it was an Argentinian player's decision to make a back-pass rather than a clearance in the second minute.

Of course, the variables that we traditionally consider important in determining results could be seen to counteract the butterfly effect; in a 90-minute match, the stronger side will win and the cream will rise, regardless of the countless potential changes in player and ball position. After all, a player reacts in real time to situations and a consistently high performing team should still create a victorious scenario. Still a very thorny issue for chaos theorists, one could argue that the individual is still free to choose their next decision, regardless of the complex tapestry of variables that carried them to that point. These arguments will inevitably lead us towards contemplation of the nature of free will itself, which will be discussed later.

But leaving the free will debate to one side for a moment, we can still see that the cream does not always rise and that those tiny decisions within a game really can have a butterfly-effect impact. We all know how unpredictable football can be, how fine the margins between victory and defeat are, and how the team that performed worse can emerge victorious. Football is not a stable system. Considering the role of psychology – impetus, confidence and determination – on the performances of teams and the outcomes of matches, it is reasonable

to assume that results, then entire tournaments, seasons, and careers, could be twisted and shaped by any single fragile and seemingly innocuous moment on a pitch.

Consider a two-footed tackle in a Premier League match that is punished by a red card. In most cases, this rush-of-blood moment could only occur given an exact intertwining of variables; the opportunity for this rash action to take place relies on the position of the players involved, the ball movement prior to it and the emotional condition of the offender (which itself is dependent upon time, status of the match, etc). It is highly unlikely that factors would have converged to this moment – and surely they would not have – had any of the variables been changed slightly. The combined effect of these variables would have fallen apart if a single player had made a single different decision between kick-off and that moment. The match could be swung by it and then the players' performances in the next few matches – defining a season and careers and so on.

It would seem, then, that chaos theory seriously undermines traditional football analysis. TR Young, in his seminal essay "Chaos Theory and the Knowledge Process", states that "the findings of chaos theory inform us that the task of the social scientist is not, cannot be, the discovery of the immutable laws of society; it is not, cannot be, to build grand theory by means of value-free research designed to approach objective reality through the method of successive approximations... For all social groups, their geometry is fractal." The complexity of the trillions of variables that affect both the individual events within a football match and the final outcome makes objective analysis of a non-linear system impossible. Does that mean all football commentary is useless?

Unfortunately, this is not the worst of it. In popular culture, chaos theory's effects are represented as pendulum moments on which our fate swings; answering a phone call, missing a train. But what is overlooked is that every single moment of our lives represents a shift in our fate and, perversely, every single moment of everybody else's lives. The football field is an excellent analogy for the world at large; the minutest changes in variables, through a knock-on effect, completely re-shape the future.

Our world can be considered as one complexly unstable system in which each of its components, in both action and inaction, affect a multitude of variables around it. Since the butterfly effect dictates that one variable has a dramatic ripple effect on future events, then, if the theory is accepted as true, clearly this is also true of every other event that has ever happened. Every motion in the universe, therefore, is inextricably intertwined with every other, by trillions of little causal threads that expand exponentially into the future, in an intricate web too complex to understand. Every event on the planet directly results from an incalculable number of variables over the past 14.7 billion years, and every event in the future will be the result of an unfathomable amount of variables all effecting quadrillions upon quadrillions more.

Consequently, our complex cause-and-effect system is mathematically predictable, even if such an equation is light years beyond the realm of possible human comprehension. Theoretically, one could analyse all of the events and variables of a given moment in time and predict exactly what would happen one second later. Since this information is now known, we could predict the next second and so on. If predicting the future is possible, then what does that say about free will? Do we live in a deterministic universe?

If this theory is to be accepted as true, then we must also accept that our attempts to predict the future based on a narrow selection of variables – such as form, ability, tactics, etc – are far too simplistic. The factors that appear to us as important, from in-game player performance to weather conditions and stadium capacity, are not a complete list. It may conform to our idealisation of sport as solid, simplistically causal and gratifyingly anti-post-modern, but it cannot be considered true.

An uncountable volume of variables, from the breakfast choice of a coach to the decisions of a person on the other side of the world, affect the future, and trillions and trillions of factors have an equal right to claim causal effect on the outcome of a match. As Young writes, "Instead of discrete object, bounded and self contained, the geometry of natural systems is more like Cantor dust, Koch curves, a Sierpenski carpet, a Menger sponge or the lovely patterns of a Mandelbrot set; such forms are riddled with holes and open to the passage of other systems... If we think of a person in fractal terms, we find a discrete object answering to the concept of the 'individual' hard to find in nature... Self and society are twin born; where a mother ends and a father starts is difficult to know. Where a mind starts and stops or meets another mind is hard to know."

Can we state with certainty that the Germany and Argentina players had any actual freedom to choose their actions on the pitch, considering the extent of the deterministically causal web they were trapped in? The reasons for receiving the ball, and the option available to them, depended upon such an intricate system of expansive chaos, one could argue that no other options could have been chosen.

Many people will argue that, in the moment, we freely choose our next decision, regardless of the fact that our scenario is conjured via an exact convergence of variables. If one believes this, then clearly the coach and analyst, dissecting a phase of play, are at least partially redeemed.

We will never be able to settle this point, although it is worth mentioning that a deeper discussion of free will in a chaos-based system would ultimately lead to questions regarding the neural pathways of the brain, the extent to which our actions are influenced by reason or impulse and the extent to which our neurological activity can itself be seen as another intricate web of cause-and-effect.

If we decide to believe in the model of determinism, as many chaos theorists do, then we would have to accept that not only is it futile to attempt to analyse the reasons for a result or predict the outcome of others, but it is also impossible to know, given the number of variables stretching back through

millennia, whether or not the action could have taken place in any other way.

And, crucially, we would find ourselves asking the question: if gazillions of interconnected phenomena led up to the moment the first ball was kicked in the World Cup final, were we incorrect to assume that either team could have won?

Of course if the result is essentially pre-determined, then we are no longer simply questioning the value of analysis, but the value of spectating altogether. Perhaps all that is left is an empty spectacle of pre-ordained moves, as sport becomes less like a battle and more like a play, a scripted performance. But would this really be problematic? Does football not already, in its grace and its artistry, resemble a theatre or a ballet performance? These are surely all questions that require serious attention.

In truth, even if free will can exist within chaos theory, we are still faced with difficult questions about the integrity of football analysis, for journalists and coaches alike. To return to Young: "[The chaos theory] view holds that nature is a seamless totality and that selection of only part of it to study necessarily results in partial knowledge. If we want to know how a particle or a system will behave, we must expand our research design to measure everything; to record more and more of reality until we have it all on paper."

It does not make sense to predict a result based on tactical suppositions, just as it does not hold true that a goal was the result of the brilliance or incompetence of an individual. On some level we may like to celebrate the unpredictability of football, but ultimately we enjoy the notion that teams and players and coaches succeed or fail for a reason. As uncomfortable as it is to accept, football – and football journalism – do not conform to the simplistic narratives we place upon them.

Perhaps what it really comes down to, when we consider the artistry and beauty of the matches themselves, is whether or not we believe this possible truth to be important.

Late Style

Taking Edward Said's theory about mature artists and applying it to Giovanni Trapattoni

By Arthur O'Dea

"Lateness is the idea of surviving beyond what is acceptable and normal."
Edward Said, *On Late Style* (2006)

"He was not the hero of our highest ideals, but he was the only hero we knew"
Augusta, Lady Gregory, "*Ireland, Real and Ideal*" (1898)

Lateness possesses a peculiar economy. Being *late* – however inconvenient – assures that you are still *being* at the very least. Once *too late*, or indeed "*the late*", and there remains scarce need for such existential soothing. Lateness signals an active participation with time, all the while reminding you of the limited nature of your relationship with time itself. Considering the artistic process as it contends with lateness as a precursor to death, Edward Said's *On Late Style* (2006) explores the "creative contradictions that often mark the late works of literary and musical artists". Rapt with concern for what the novelist Jack London described as the "last panic" before the "most satisfying sleep", the artist, consumed now with a tangible sense of exile, slips from the "established social order of which [they] are a part." Consequentially understood as a creative period of "late style", the environment in which these new works are developed enhances the sense that what we are witnessing is

something in "direct contrast to what is *popular* (acceptable) *at the time*". It is this juxtaposition between the popular, the ageing artist and his unexpected, misunderstood works that generates such intrigue for the study of "late style".

Although Said was not the first to query this "late" disposition, *On Late Style* provided the definitive take on this phenomenon in a broad, compendious book format. A Palestinian academic educated at the prestigious North American universities of Yale and Princeton, his own well-documented sense of exile – his autobiography *Out Of Place* lending something to this assertion in title alone – primed his eventual understanding and interpretation for what became of so many great artists in their concluding years. Calling upon scholarly concerns that stretched beyond his vociferous support for Palestinian equality, the results of this posthumously published text on lateness and late style signifies an irrefutable advance in our attempts to understand this odd, yet familiar occurrence.

The parameters of Said's investigation, however, maintained a largely classical scope. This was no oversight. Pairing off "late style" with "popular culture" was not necessarily intended ever to become part of the procedure. It is a decision we may now contend with, though. Ushering "late style" into a contemporary setting will, admittedly, require minor adjustments to the framework Said initially suggests with *On Late Style*. Yet with football in particular – though it is extremely doubtful Said would have approved – "late style" can flourish with many of the Saidian conventions still in play. Addressing Giovanni Trapattoni's reign as the national manager of the Republic of Ireland football team, we have a pairing of "late style" and football that will constitute what I hope will become the beginning of a broader discussion in terms of where football and "late style" may covalence; the question of "late style" and football players – as opposed to the more easily distinguished role of manager – being the natural critical development. Initially, however, concern about the terminology of this particular study must be addressed.

While football and "late style" are as yet unacquainted, the singular qualities of "late" and "style" possess footballing connotations that necessitate some prior clarification. Lateness in football tends to concern a period of late excitement or drama in a match or season – "Agüero-oooooooooooo" being a rare example of both. As a mechanism of grander conclusion, discussions of lateness tend to circulate the perceived unsuitability of a player or manager to remain in situ. On the rare occasion where lateness meets football at the actual juncture of death or devastation, football, like Said's understanding of art, remains immune, having never been "alive" in the first place. Death in football can usually be read as signification of retirement, enforced or otherwise. Football, like art, cannot be *late*. The development of

these qualities is entirely down to the individuals involved.

With the onus on individuality, we thus come to consider style. Including, but not limited to, a "style" of playing football in a tactical/impulsive sense, the individual in possession of style tends to be of great intrigue to us, if not quite always in an adulatory sense – the perceived disparity between José Mourinho and Pep Guardiola as managers of Real Madrid and Barcelona respectively, conformed to a wide ranging encapsulation of what fans both sought and in turn deplored about the understood style of how both clubs operated. Style, in opposition to skill or ability alone, registers its appeal in terms of how it is received and interpreted – the "late" intrigue afforded to Andrea Pirlo being a telling example of how a *very good* player (not great in the sense of Francesco Totti – but this is for a later discussion) can generate popular momentum on the basis of how he wears a beard, takes a penalty or hits a ten-yard pass. For the purpose of investigating "late style" and football, the understanding afforded to both words will seek to conjure the broader, Saidian determination of what occurs when this reliability on/attraction toward style becomes entrenched in a misunderstood period of lateness.

What, then, of Giovanni Trapattoni, the Irish national side and the suitability of this pairing to demonstrate the deployment of "late style" unto football? Located within the practicalities of his appointment, his apparent unwillingness to learn English, his relentless refusal to placate an overwhelming public desire to witness certain un-picked players in action, the detached, stand-offish approach to communication he demonstrated with both players and the media, and, perhaps most importantly, a team-selection policy which regimentally upheld what he understood to be Ireland's obvious footballing deficiencies, Trapattoni's concluding years are rife with the intransigence Said foresaw as essential to a "late style."

Arriving as an undisputed doyen of club management with big sides, the Irish position initially bestowed upon him a scenario verging on "world-class". In the wake of the disastrous Steve Staunton era (the Euro 2008 qualifying campaign), Trapattoni inherited a squad of good players (Given, Keane, Duff, Dunne *et al.*) that had been lacking guidance and were vastly under-performing as a result. The initial remit of this position was that of a trouble-shooting role in which any improvement on the 14-goals-against, 10-points-adrift-of-second-place shambles that had constituted Staunton's sole campaign in charge would be measured as a success.

On this expectation Trapattoni undisputedly delivered. Yet, improving upon Staunton's efforts constituted a managerial expectation capable of being achieved by a figure of far smaller stature than Giovanni Trapattoni. Such a manager may not have commanded a €2 million annual salary. Under the auspices of his appointment, did the great Trapattoni actually advance Irish football in any tangible, long-term sense? Arguably, once he had found a way of consolidating a highly structured, technically indifferent defensive unit, no, he did not appear too concerned with what may naturally be assumed to be

the next obvious destination for thought: attack. With the controversy of the Thierry Henry handball overshadowing Ireland's failure to qualify for the World Cup, Trapattoni's opening campaign did not immediately receive the wide-ranging level of doubt and scepticism it probably deserved. The seeds of what can now be identified as the intricacies of Trapattoni's "late style" can be seen to flourish in his subsequent efforts at qualification (Euro 2012 and the 2014 World Cup). That November evening in Paris will be looked upon only briefly as a manner of elucidating Trapattoni's liberation from the expectancies surrounding Ireland's relatively "golden generation."

With occasional reference to "the wife", the football manager, or "husband", identifies the "crack ... that [allows] the light in" (Leonard Cohen, "Anthem"). Indicative of a family life that cannot coincide publicly with the demands of football management, it bears fruit in allowing our enhanced understanding of what may drive the manager's career decisions. Paola Trapattoni, wife to Giovanni since 1964, is quoted throughout Egon Theiner's and Elisabeth Schlammerl's *Trapattoni – A Life in Football*. The voice of reason concerning Trapattoni's relentless managerial career and the limitations it placed on the relationships he may have otherwise cultivated with his children and grandchildren, his "personal" justification for taking on the Ireland role at 69 lay with the possibility of spending "a lot more time ... with my family." At an age when most have already slowed down, Trapattoni undertook his fourth foreign expedition in as many years. Subjectively, as his case cannot be understood in any sense of normality, that Trapattoni would even suggest a degree of reining in his absolute commitment to this latest role is certainly unique. Given the unchartered domain of football and "late style", this admitted attempt to merge his footballing "obsession" with the responsibilities of his home life suggests an alteration in his approach that attempts to contend with the reality that time is elapsing perhaps a little faster now. In truth, much of what would constitute Trapattoni's "late style" can be rooted back to this initial intention to take a step back while still moving ceaselessly forward. As shall be shown, his cavalier attitude toward the English language in particular demonstrated one such area in which Trapattoni attempts to remain somewhat unavailable.

Spells working in Germany, Portugal and Austria had not previously left Trapattoni capable of carrying out his professional speaking duties without the aid of an interpreter. Speaking on his return to Bayern Munich in 1996, Trapattoni suggested that his improved mastery of the German language would now allow for "Trapattoni at 100%." Yet, while this second spell at Bayern certainly signalled an improvement on his first encounter two years previously, the infamous "Strunz" press-conference of March 1998 went some way toward demonstrating how much he had still to learn linguistically. Having never managed in Italy after his disappointing Euro 2004 campaign in charge of the *Azzurri*, issues with language tend perhaps to illuminate why his subsequent roles with Stuttgart, Benfica and RB Salzburg only made it as far as a second season (coincidentally or not, the multi-lingual Lothar Matthäus

was his assistant in this final club role). One may ponder what thus distinguishes his ultimate issues with the English language and the Irish job as a "late" concern. Primarily, he would persist with this Irish role for a whole year longer than his previous three foreign jobs combined. Speaking in September 2013, two days prior to his eventual leaving the Ireland role, Trapattoni ventured to suggest that John Delaney, the CEO of the FAI, should realistically say, "Giovanni continue because Giovanni make great job." Although most Irish listeners may have taken great umbrage to what Trapattoni understood as a "great job", five years in an English-speaking role that allowed for quite a lot of free time should have enabled a greater learning effort on Trapattoni's part. Yes, even though he was by then a septuagenarian approaching his fifth decade of football management, an era of heavily saturated football analysis and a vast media presence did not allow Trapattoni's unwillingness/incapability to learn pass by without external judgement. The great tenacity with which he carried out this role dissuades the suggestion that laziness or complacency may have become an issue. Trapattoni cared considerably, but his willingness to engage seemed to be severely waning. He was no longer concerned with "Trapattoni at 100%" as it had once been understood. This would be granted unfortunate clarity in his later dealings − both public and private − with Irish players young and old.

What strikes one as symptomatic of "late style" is Trapattoni's apparent acceptance to *remain* mis-understood, however. Not shy by nature, his inability to communicate articulately made him somewhat less culpable for what may or may not go wrong. His sustained successes in previous years did not encourage doubt in terms of the man's intellect, ingenuity or managerial ability. Yet, in limiting his available vocabulary (safe also in the knowledge presumably that his ceaseless interpreter Manuela Spinelli would tidy up any particularly impulsive Italian comments he did make) Trapattoni could temper expectation and, for better or worse (usually worse, sadly), allow his team to do the talking. This was not a luxury that could possibly have been afforded to him previously. The exilic nature of Beethoven's late creativity as discussed in *On Late Style* echoes somewhat the isolation Trapattoni sought while working on his final "masterpiece". Beethoven's absolute deafness in the later years of his life granted a degree of critical immunity from the unusual works he was constructing. Trapattoni, albeit more willingly, assumed a veneer of silence intended to limit how involved he need be with his own public relations. The contrary nature of his initial approach and attitude to the managerial role in Ireland would undeniably shape the *late* differences that would distinguish Trapattoni's "late style".

"Trapattoni let them off the leash" Eamonn Dunphy, speaking in wake of Ireland's play-off defeat to France, November 2009.

To those for whom watching Ireland play is an incomplete experience without the analysis of John Giles, Liam Brady and Eamonn Dunphy, RTÉ's football panellists, the critical response to the 2009 play-off loss to France was one of cautious optimism. Weary though many had become with Ireland's reserved playing approach under Trapattoni, the superb performance in Paris – relatively, at least – was understood to be a true sampling of Ireland's potential. Having constructed a degree of solidity so desperately absent throughout the short-lived Staunton era, it was assumed that the prowess displayed in Paris would encourage Trapattoni to develop such attacking instincts. In truth, it would be the last performance of its kind from Trapattoni's Ireland.

Of concern also for the panel that evening – Graeme Souness was filling in for Liam Brady, who was working for Trapattoni within the Ireland set-up at this time – was Trapattoni's perceived approach to scouting and player recruitment. Citing the relentless efforts of then England manager Fabio Capello to witness first-hand as many potential players as possible, Trapattoni's understood reliance upon watching video recordings of players instead was pilloried as not being good enough. Trapattoni, unlike Capello and his backroom staff, never did move closer to the country that supplied most of his potential players. Indicative perhaps of a mentality which suggested that Ireland's pool of players was so shallow as to make the possibility of overlooking any worthwhile player near impossible, Trapattoni's approach instead definitively reflected the limitations he wished to inflict tactically. It is doubtful whether the players Trapattoni required for this system necessarily needed to be observed first-hand prior to selection.

Much can be deduced of Trapattoni's intransigent approach to football from his most consistent central midfield pairing in an age in which Barcelona and Spain in particular were renewing the idea of valuing possession of the ball. Both Keith Andrews (28) and Glenn Whelan (24) were made full Irish internationals under Trapattoni. With scant Premier League experience, such a decision suggests that the degree of consideration Trapattoni brought to his scouting and recruitment still had the potential to be effective, if not revelatory. However, what cannot be shaken is the ultimate understanding that in seeking a central midfield pairing hell-bent on defending, the capabilities of Andrews/Whelan made perfect sense. Unlike established creative midfielders such as Andy Reid, Keith Fahey and Wes Hoolahan who would remain predominantly ostracised throughout the Trapattoni era, players distinctly lacking that impulsivity possible of winning a game were recruited instead for their ability and willingness to conform blindly. Reid, Fahey and Hoolahan would play no part for Ireland at Euro 2012; Paul Green, unattached, would get ten minutes against Spain. Although the solidity promised by Andrews/Whelan was a welcome development, the strictness of Trapattoni's functionality encouraged an exceptionally basic approach that ultimately left Ireland without possession of the ball more often than not. But for the individual brilliance of Richard Dunne and Robbie Keane, Euro 2012 qualification from a group containing Russia, Slovakia, Armenia, FYR Macedonia and Andorra would have been highly unlikely.

As a demonstration of his "late style", Trapattoni's recruitment policy does not appear complacent; rather it is inherently limited in the parameters it worked under. As is often the case with "late style", Trapattoni's decision-making was ultimately mis-understood. If he had the wherewithal to locate some of those who would make an international breakthrough during his tenure, it is highly unlikely that Trapattoni did not know what those more publicly acceptable players could bring to his side. "Late style" encourages this sense of confusion and apparent stagnation to become a prevalent factor. In contrast to his Juventus hey-day in the seventies and eighties, he seemed resistant to individual prowess with his Irish side. Whereas at Juventus Michel Platini had epitomised the highpoint of capability that rendered Trapattoni's strict stylisation a perfect foundation in which to flourish, Ireland's creative element was never nourished in this regard — it relied entirely upon the defensive structuring. Trapattoni simply appeared to have absolutely no faith in Ireland's ability to retain the ball and build accordingly. Entitled as he was to approach this role as he saw fit, Trapattoni's systematic rigidity was so averse to the varying ideals of football at this time that it cannot be looked upon as anything other than a peculiar pattern of his "late style".

Jack Charlton's Ireland of the late eighties and early nineties similarly advocated an approach that didn't necessarily consider possession of the ball all that valuable. Their resulting successes were wrought in an environment in which Irish fans had never before witnessed the realities of tournament qualification. One would be mistaken for assuming that the furore surrounding Ireland's participation in Italia 90 was solely a football affair. Of the five games Ireland played, their only "win" came in the last-16 penalty shoot-out against Romania[1]. Having subsequently experienced two more World Cups – the 2002 Roy Keane v Mick McCarthy situation leaving it as the great "What If?" for Ireland's football fans – Trapattoni inherited a nation that was no longer content with merely being there – however misplaced such confidence may have been on occasion. With more access to global football than ever before, Ireland's followers could not fathom why such a negative approach was to be upheld at all times. Though a degree of success was certainly rendered in qualifying for Euro 2012, no sooner had Poland quietened down as the Irish fans departed than the business of such an abysmal showing on the pitch required explaining. As would be displayed by the personnel chosen to undertake qualification for the 2014 World Cup, clarity was not forthcoming from Trapattoni.

Trapattoni's reluctance to adapt and develop his Irish team in any meaningful, progressive manner remains the fundamental tenet of his "late style". Having prided himself previously on his introduction of the 19-year old Alessandro Del Piero to the Juventus team during his second spell in charge in the early nineties, Trapattoni's reserved approach to the Irish youth bears some thinking about. Seamus Coleman, James McCarthy and James McClean are not necessarily cut from the same cloth as Del Piero.

Yet, relative to that which Ireland can hope to expect it is quite unusual that three such players have yet to acquire a combined total of 100 caps. While Trapattoni may well have anticipated their involvement in years to come, it is somewhat facetious to assume that he had Ireland's long-term interests in heart when dealing with these players while under his tutelage. They, and a select few more, were afforded very limited realistic opportunities to develop internationally. Although in McCarthy's case a family bereavement halted his opportunity to attend Euro 2012, 14 minutes was the total amount of playing time afforded to McClean. Coleman did not even make the squad.

Trapattoni's unwillingness to blood Ireland's younger – arguably more exciting and better also – players proved only more irritating and unusual when one considers his work with those he deemed more suitable. One cannot overlook the fact that at times players like Liam Lawrence, Caleb Folan and, perhaps most impressively, Jon Walters were introduced to the Irish side with very little fuss and an occasionally solid return. Vitalising the inner underdog and frustrations of those Irish players who had never previously considered international football a likely manifestation, the "late" Trapattoni – somewhat akin to Beethoven as per Theodor Adorno – can be seen "catching fire between extremes". The "lost totality" that now pervades his work does not allow for a consistent demonstration of his capabilities; only brief flashes

---

[1] *See Dion Fanning's "Booze Boys" in Issue Eleven of* The Blizzard *for an acute observation of the extra-curricular appeals of that summer.*

of brilliance. Sensing Trapattoni's ultimate concern with time, however, it would appear that in search of instant gratification he simply did not wish to disrupt the stability harnessed with the introduction of a youthful 'wild-card'. The self-imposed exile he sought to work in left him scant room for the true consideration of alternatives. At club level, such immediacy and a reluctance to trust is usually necessary under the premise of a looming relegation. Ireland after Staunton certainly provides an international sampling of such dire straits. It simply is not feasible, however, to maintain the approach that staved off "relegation" as you are trying subsequently to move forward. Epitomising the very lateness he was so acutely aware of, Trapattoni's stubborn approach to player development was not the correct decision when one decided to hold down an international position for five years. If not for player retirements, it is highly likely that the team he started off with in May 2008 in a friendly against Serbia would have mirrored somewhat the last Ireland side he would send out five years on. As was acutely captured by the *Guardian's* Paul Doyle upon Trapattoni's eventual departure: "[He was] a manager who remained stubborn enough to believe that things would turn out as he foresaw no matter what was unfolding before his eyes." The truth of this statement surely came to its truest fulfilment in the disastrous summer of Euro 2012. That so very little would change – least of all the manager – before the beginning of Ireland's attempts at qualifying for the 2014 World Cup says more perhaps of Ireland than it does of this "late" Trapattoni.

The negativity which constitutes the body of this article allows for the assumption that "late style" is in essence a "bad" occurrence. Trapattoni arrived, consolidated defensively and thus continued flogging this same defensive agenda until it ceased entirely against Sweden and then Austria in September 2013. If this was "late style", where exactly did the "constructive" element of the late works Said spoke of emerge during Trapattoni's tenure? Unsurprisingly, the most compelling case for a "constructive" element can be made with relation to Trapattoni's improvement of Ireland's defensive capabilities. Seamus Coleman, a player entitled to resent Trapattoni for his often inexplicable exclusion from the Italian's starting XI, made public in late 2014 his admiration for Trapattoni with relation to how he had "learned a lot from him on the defensive side of things."

Quoting Adorno's thoughts on the late Beethoven, Said's *On Late Style* makes reference to the almost "unabashedly primitive" music Beethoven created in this period. For Trapattoni too, one cannot but look to his tactical approach with Ireland and wonder at what point he forgot, lost or overruled the element of such a defensive outlook that enables an attacking motion to develop. Possessing many of the elements which had granted his Juventus and Internazionale sides such wonderful success, the *late* Trapattoni appeared to foresee international football with a minor nation to be mostly a case of winning the "gimmes" and not losing the rest. In this regard he may well have tapped into an underlying truth of a qualifying layout that attempts to harbour the ambitions of some 50 or so teams. While his approach was not unique, the manner of success rendered from it over three campaigns puts Trapattoni more or less on par with Ireland's second most successful manager, Mick McCarthy – and to be fair, he had Roy Keane right up until the tide began to turn. Trapattoni's "late style" brought far more aggravation and boredom for a footballing community that was becoming swayed by the easy success of supporting the rugby alternative. From a supporter's point of view, witnessing a team led by a manager in the throes of a "late style" is unlikely to be an exciting time. That "late style" requires intransigence, difficulty and unresolved contradiction to develop does little to placate the appeal most have for a good standard of attacking football. Adorno surmised that the "late works are the catastrophes." A true reflection perhaps of how many felt about Trapattoni's late style of football, there is no other way around the fact that late and unpleasant as it often was it yet remained *football* in a somewhat more contorted form.

142

Austria

"Everybody said, "It's super"
and "Keep going.""

Restoring the Glory

Austria's coach Marcel Koller explains their first tournament qualification in 18 years

By Vladimir Novak

When the Swiss coach Marcel Koller was appointed Austria manager in October 2011, there was widespread scepticism. He had taken St Gallen and Grasshoppers to the Swiss title, but the most recent of those successes had come in 2003, since when he'd done nothing more than lead Bochum into the Bundesliga. When Koller took over, Austria were 70th in the Fifa rankings. They've since climbed into the top 20 and have guaranteed their place at Euro 2016. He's transformed one of Europe's great underachievers into a winning team that plays attractive football.

⊕ *When you were a player and later a coach in Switzerland and Germany, what was your impression of Austrian football?*

I scored my first goal for the [Switzerland] national team against Austria, past Franz Wohlfahrt, who until recently was my goalkeeping coach. I knew that Austria always had very good players in the past, like Herbert Prohaska. More recently I noticed that they had a fine national team and after I was offered the Austria job, I gathered information to see if this project could work out well.

⊕ *Austrian football has a great tradition, with successes of the Wunderteam in the 1930, then in the 1950s, and to a*

certain extent in the 1970s. However, over the past 30 years there was a big decline. What happened?

It's difficult to say. To be honest, I'd never really looked into why things hadn't gone so well for Austrian football and I also think that it's not my job to talk about it. For me it was important to analyse the current state of things before I agreed to take the job, to convince myself about the potential of this team and about the prospects of achieving progress with those players, to see if they could play according to my philosophy. For the time being, things have worked out well and it looks as though I made the right decision.

⊕ *After you received the offer to take over the Austria national team, what was your first thought?*

I thought that it was an interesting job and I wanted to check whether the players had quality. I was wondering if my ideas about football were realisable with those players.

⊕ *Austria have failed to qualify for five major tournaments in a row. Apart from Euro 2008, when Austria were a co-host, their last participation at a major tournament was at the World Cup in France in 1998. You were taking over an underdog: was that an additional motivation – the chance to restore past glories?*

No, not really. It's always difficult to predict how things will work out. I know how to reach the players. I know how I like to train and what my ideas look like, how I can transfer those ideas to the players. But you can't know in advance if or how everything will click, because there can be many obstacles. Therefore, first you have to start working and at first you don't know if the players will respond, if they can process everything you ask them to do. Basically at the beginning everything is theory, while the praxis is much more difficult – to get there where we are actually now. For now everything in functioning well and our aim is to continue like that.

How did it go in the first months? What did you discover, diagnose and what was your plan to progress?

At first it was a bit difficult, because it was the first time that I'd worked as national coach. I had to develop our project although I only had the players with me for a short time. We had our first game in November 2011 [a 2-1 defeat in friendly away to Ukraine] and then my next contact with the players wasn't until February 2012 [a 3-1 win over Finland] and then in late May, early June [3-2 against Ukraine]. You have to develop things in theory and travel to the players. I made many trips, visiting the players at their clubs. I had talks with the players. I had to transmit my philosophy to them and I wanted to do this as quickly as possible. The only way to do it was to travel around and visit the players. At the same time I followed league games, both

in Austria and in foreign leagues where national team players were.

At the beginning it was obvious that many people, many fans were moaning, that they were always unhappy about something, always quick to criticise. I took it in my own way. Basically I'm very positive and I didn't hesitate to talk to people who moaned. I put many things through a filter, but I also tried to see what could be useful from all those opinions and remarks. I noticed that it took a year before those things disappeared. I noticed that nobody moaned any more. Instead, when I was on the street or in stadiums, people greeted me in a friendly way and asked for pictures and autographs. They no longer said, "This and that is bad, you have to do this and that." Instead everybody was giving me thumbs up, everybody said, "It's super" and "Keep going."

Do you think that one could say that you took on the job without any great risk, that you were in a win-win situation? If Austria again failed to qualify, it wouldn't have been anything new, but if you did qualify, it would be regarded as a great achievement?

Well, I see that a bit differently. After all, we did not qualify for the World Cup [in 2014], even though we were close to reaching the play-off. Back then the Austrian football federation (ÖFB) could have said, "Okay, we'll try another coach." So, I don't think that it was a win-win situation. However, the ÖFB and I agreed to continue together. That was important, because I said back then that two years is too short a period for a national coach to implement his ideas. The players and I needed more time to train together, I needed more time to transmit our tactics to them. I always said that I needed more time with the national team to develop things. Well, now the fruits of our joint work are there and we hope that it will stay like that.

✥ What is your coaching philosophy?

Away from the pitch, I think that there needs to be respect and decency, to have a good relationship. And if there is not a good relationship, to tackle the problem, to talk about it and to try to sort it out. On the pitch I like my team to be active. I don't like to sit back and wait for the opponent to make a mistake. I want to participate actively in the game, and that also means when we don't have the ball. On the one hand to try to get back possession as quickly as possible and on the other hand, when we have the ball, I want us to try to play football − with a lot of technique, a lot of running and a lot of intensity to impose our offensive play.

✥ Did it bother you that at first a lot of people didn't accept you?

No, it didn't bother me. Because I knew that most of them didn't know me well. They just quickly trumpeted their views, maybe without thinking too much about it. Perhaps some of them had individual agendas. But I knew that I had to start my work and I was convinced that with those players I could have success. And that's more important than being unhappy about somebody's quotes.

✥ Since then, all of them have apologised: Herbert Prohaska, Hans Krankl, Toni Polster... All of them praised your work in the highest terms. What can you say about that? Did they also apologise personally?

[Laughs]. No, not all of them have apologised. But that's irrelevant. Prohaska [a former player who is the main pundit on Austrian national TV] apologised through the media. He said that he made a mistake, that it was a wrong judgment. But that's not an issue. It doesn't bother me and it won't be a burden for me.

✥ Not only in Austria but also elsewhere, some people say that the national team is a national affair and that it's not ideal to have a foreign coach. What do you make of it?

I have an open mind about that. I remember that we in Switzerland at one point had a long period when we didn't qualify for major tournaments. I was a player at that time and then we had foreign coaches with the national team. Firstly Uli Stielike, who made a big contribution to Switzerland making a step forward. Then [for USA 94] with Roy Hodgson we qualified for the first time for 28 years. So, it doesn't mean that it's bad to have a foreigner as national coach. He must be a good coach - that's the decisive factor, not his nationality.

✥ What about the rivalry between neighbours Switzerland and Austria? In alpine skiing it's huge. What about football?

Well, here and there maybe there's the odd bit of teasing, especially in western Austria near the Swiss border. In football in recent years the Austria national team was usually behind Switzerland, but we are now trying to tickle them a little bit and to overtake them.

✥ During your career as player you had two successful qualifying campaigns with Switzerland [for USA 94 and Euro

96]. Did that experience play a role in your work with the Austria national team? Were you able to transmit something from your own experiences to your players?

No, I wouldn't say that this played a role. Of course, the experiences one collects as player are valuable for a coaching career. But when you are a player, you are not that deeply involved in the whole process of what the coach is doing. As player you arrive in the national team and everything is set up. You don't have to worry about anything else, but to try to put in your best performance for the team. I was very happy to be part of the team at Euro 96 [Koller missed World Cup USA 94 through an injury], because I knew that afterwards I would retire from international football and it was a really beautiful experience to play at a major tournament.

⚽ *It's an eternal question for national coaches whether they should select players who are in good form, who are regulars at their clubs, or stick to a core of players, build good team-play, even if that means using players with little or no playing time. You've trusted some players who were not regulars at their clubs. What's your argument for that?*

I think that this is an individual decision. It depends on how national coaches look at that question. For me the most important thing is that I have to be convinced about the football qualities a player has. If that player in his foreign club is not always playing, because of a lot of competition in that squad, it doesn't necessarily mean that he is not in good form. We keep such players in the national team, because we know

their quality and because we know that they can help us. That's why we selected them in the first place. Of course it's an advantage if a player has lot of playing time at his club, if he's at full rhythm all the time, if he has the 90 minutes in his legs, because sometimes you notice lack of power after 60 or 70 minutes, and then you have to do something. But, as I said, the main reason I select a player is his football quality, regardless of his situation in his club.

⚽ *How do you get along with the Austrian mentality? They say that Austrians are quickly satisfied. "It's okay like that" and "We shall see" are supposed to be characteristic Austrian attitudes. Did you see that mentality in your work with the national team? How did you handle it?*

Yes, that's the mentality of many Austrians. If you have your holidays here, then you'll like it. But when you work together and when you want to have success, it's important not to be satisfied too easily and not to lean back. We talked about this in our team meetings and we made it clear that we did not want 80% but 100% in each game. It took some time until we reached 100% and it's important to demand it, to remind the players of that. But I'm happy to say that we've reached a point at which the players have recognised for themselves that it's better always to give 100%. They've realised that we have success. Everything is more pleasant when you have success. So I'm glad that we managed to sort this out.

⚽ *Like many national teams and clubs, you have a psychologist in your backroom staff. What can you say about the role of Thomas Graw?*

While I was a player and also later when I started working as coach, I was always interested in psychology. A coach has to cope with a huge number of things; he has to have everything under control. Therefore I think it's very important to have a good coaching team, to have co-workers who can take over some tasks from the coach. When I worked at Bochum, I began to work with Thomas and I noticed that it's very important that the players do not always have to address the coach when they have some problem. Actually, in such situations, players tend to avoid talking to the coach, because they fear that he won't put them in the team. Therefore it's good that they have another guy for a confidential chat. So far it's worked very well. Those are individual talks, which are not compulsory, but the players use them, not only during a national team get-together, but also while they are with their clubs.

And what's the task of the sports scientist Dr Gerhard Zallinger?

He works in the field of physiology. He's in charge of performance data and analysis in conditioning. He puts together individual programs for the players, particularly if a player is not always a regular at his club. In such cases we are in contact with the player and we ask him to do additional training to be at the required level when he comes to the national team.

Before you signed a new contract with the ÖFB in autumn 2013, you had an offer to take over the Switzerland national team. Did you have a dilemma because of the call of your home country – is that why it took you a long time to accept the Austria extension?

I wouldn't say that it took me a long time. For media two or three days is an extremely long time. After we came back from the Faroe Islands, after our last World Cup qualifier, I said in a press conference that we would have contract talks and that this would not be finished from today to tomorrow. Eventually the talks lasted for around one week, if I remember rightly. The Austrian media exaggerated in their reports. I needed time to make a decision. When your home country calls you to become national coach, I think it's normal that you think about it, whether it would be the right decision or not to take over the Swiss national team. I was very happy in Austria. At that point I had already lived in Vienna for two years. Actually, the main thing was the question of whether I could continue with the Austria national team. Then I also thought that I was talking all the time about how two years were not enough with a national team, and if I left Austria and took over Switzerland, I would have to start all over again. I would have to start from zero. Of course I also realised that with this Austria team there was the possibility for progress, that the potential was there, that their players showed the desire to go on, and that the fans were positive. At the same time I had also great support from the ÖFB as well as from the fans in Austria, everybody there asked me to stay. So I made the decision to continue with Austria and, well, so far I haven't regretted it.

On taking the Austria job you said that it could take years until your coaching handwriting could be identified. It seems now that you can see your handwriting. How would you describe it? What kind of stamp have you managed to imprint

on the playing style of the Austria national team?

Those who've known me for a long time can say, "Okay, that's Marcel Koller who plays here." On the one hand it's aggressive play in defending, but it's also the creative play in attacking actions. You can see it if you follow me for a long time. Also it's the manner in which I handle things, how I like to follow my goals, that it's not easy to make me change my path when I'm convinced that it's the right direction. Sometimes there is some resistance, but I can cope with it.

⊕ *In the World Cup qualifiers for Brazil 2014 you had that crucial game in Sweden when a draw would have been enough to get to the play-off. You played well and had a 1-0 lead, but in the end you lost 2-1. Now, two years later, this probably would not happen. Do you agree?*

Yes, absolutely. You need games like that to analyse afterwards where the mistakes were made when we were under pressure. And then you can try to correct things. We conceded late goals and now we have it in our heads how we have to play when we have a 1-0 lead and there's 10 minutes until the end of the game. We showed that in the game against Russia [a 1-0 victory in Moscow in early June in a Euro qualifier].

⊕ *Between that 2-1 defeat in Sweden and the resounding 4-1 win in Sweden two years later, what has changed?*

Back in 2013 we dominated in the first half and we showed some fantastic play. But in the second half we failed to continue in that style. This time it was different. We put in a consistent performance throughout the whole game and – especially in the second half – we had chances to score even more goals. The shortest way to describe the development is that the team has become more mature and more clever.

⊕ *What went through your head in those moments after such a spectacular performance?*

The whole pressure of qualifying fell away. It was clear that "we'd done it". It was an amazing liberating and beautiful moment. And in addition to that, after such a high-level performance of the team. It made me very proud – and grateful, because the players and the entire coaching staff had worked very hard to reach such a moment.

⊕ *On paper, taking first place ahead of Russia and Sweden was a surprise. Can Austria deliver another surprise at Euro 2016? What result would you be happy with in France?*

The first place is an answer to the doubters, who otherwise would have said that we qualified only because the number of participants has been increased from 16 to 24 teams. For me first place is not a surprise, because I know about the potential of this team.

⊕ *The day after the win in Sweden, you came to your press-conference wearing a beret and eating a baguette. Whose idea was that?*

It was my idea. Already in March this year I showed up with that costume in front of the team and I told the players,

"This is our destination". After we wrapped up the qualifications, I could do it also in public.

🔄 *Naturalised players in national teams: yes or no? Would you pick a Brazilian with an Austrian passport?*

Well, unlike in other sports, you can't effectively just buy players for the national team. There is the rule that a player has to live and play in that country for five years, and only then he can change citizenship and be eligible to play for the national team, if he's player we need. If that did happen, if everything was okay, if that player had the necessary quality, and he identified with his new country, then that question would probably be on the agenda and I would be open to such an option.

🔄 *Do you have in your plans some new, young and talented players who could make it to the squad for Euro 2016?*

Yes, we have some youngsters. For example [Philipp] Schobesberger from Rapid [Vienna] was with us for the first time for the Russia game. We have [Valentino] Lazaro, who has unfortunately been injured. [Marcel] Sabitzer is also a young player, who has already been with us a while. Of course it needs time for them to adapt to the team, until they put in constant and good performances. We will continue looking for new players. We will call them up to the national team, to see how they will settle in the new environment, to give them an opportunity to see the friendliness among their team-mates, to let them sniff the atmosphere in the national team. Ⓑ

The Burden of History

For years, Austrian football has been struggling to live up to its glorious past

By Peter Linden

A 20-year wait between the soaring heights of Austrian football – evidently that is part of the experience. The Austrian football federation (ÖFB) turned 111 this year and has gone through a lot in its existence. There were triumphs in the 1930s with the world-renowned *Wunderteam*'s series of wins under Hugo Meisl.

That side was born on 16 May 1931 when Meisl slammed a piece of paper with his selection for the match against Scotland on a table at the Ring-Café, a coffee house on the Stubenring in Vienna frequented mainly by sports journalists. They had talked Meisl round to bringing back the duo of Matthias Sindelar and Fritz Gschweidl. The 5-0 defeat of the Scots was the beginning of a great era of success between May 1931 and February 1933: 6-0 and 5-0 against Germany, 8-1 against Switzerland, 2-1 against Italy, 6-1 against Belgium, 4-0 against France, 8-2 against the "archenemy" Hungary. Even the 4-3 defeat against England at Stamford Bridge didn't put an end to the hymns of praise. One line from the brawny defender Karl Sesta is still legendary 83 years later. At the team's presentation the British king told him, "You have a wonderful profession as a footballer." Sesta's retort was, ***"Sie haben a ka schlechte Hack'n, Majestät."*** ["Your gig isn't bad either, majesty," in Viennese dialect]. But at the 1934 World

Cup seven players from the ***Wunderteam*** were missing. The dire economic situation had a catastrophic impact on World Cup preparations. In the semi-final, Austria lost 1-0 to Italy thanks to a controversial goal. The match for third place, played in washed-out kits borrowed from AC Napoli, was lost 3-2 to Germany – the birth of the decades-long "German complex".

Winning silver at the Olympics in Berlin in 1936 with an amateur team was a sensation. On 28 March 1938 the Austrian Football Association (ÖFB) ceased to exist. The organisation was liquidated and transferred to the *Deutscher Reichsbund für Leibesübungen, Fachamt Fußball* [German Federation for Physical Education, Football Office] in Charlottenburg, Berlin.

During this difficult time Rapid sent strong signs of life from Vienna. In 1941, victory in the German Cup final against Schalke on June 22 in front of 100,000 spectators at the Olympiastadion in Berlin. After being 3-0 down, with four goals in nine minutes. Three of them by the famous marksman Bimbo Binder. On the same day as Germany declared war on Russia.

Four and a half years later, on 6 December 1945, the first post-war international was played on Viennese soil, with Vienna still divided by the four occupying powers. The aged Fifa president Jules Rimet graced it with his presence. With a 4-1 win against France, Austria sealed their return to the international football family. In the absence of a new national anthem the band struck up the rousing march *"Oh, du mein Österreich"* ["Oh my Austria"]. Two years later, a highlight: a 5-1 win in Vienna over the double World Cup-winners Italy. Talents such as the goalkeeper Zeman, Ernst Happel, the brothers Alfred and Robert Körner, Stojaspal, Wagner, Hanappi and the famous Ernst Ocwirk showed, as it were, the resurrection from the rubble and the chaos of the post-war period, from which emerged a successful team. Their third place at the World Cup in Switzerland was the biggest success to date. As an incentive, the players were promised they could move abroad after the World Cup.

The quarter-final in front of 60,000 spectators in Lausanne against Switzerland is still one of the craziest games in Word Cup history. 7-5 in a heated battle. After 18 minutes, 3-0 to Switzerland; after 34 minutes, 6-4 to Austria; two minutes later only 6-5. The goalkeeper Kurt Schmied suffering from heatstroke in the sweltering temperature before half-time. There were no substitutions. He had to persevere in a trance-like state, staggered between his posts without being able to control his reflexes, didn't know the score. Next to one post stood the team masseur, conducting him, throwing him soaking wet sponges as refreshment, shouting excitedly, "Kurtl, watch out! They're coming!" With a lot of luck Austria made

it through. For the semi-final in Basel, Zeman was in goal, for the black day against Germany. The 6-1 defeat was considered the biggest debacle in the history of Austrian football and Zeman and Happel had to serve as scapegoats. Some newspapers even claimed that Austria had been bribed by a German industrialist. In Zurich, they succeeded in repairing their reputation with a 3-1 win against Uruguay, in which Ocwirk excelled. The World Cup heroes returned home to a huge reception, carried out of the Westbahnhof in Vienna on the crowd's shoulders. The prize for third place: not even €3000 in today's currency.

In 1958 came a Swedish disappointment. Without a win, Austria bade farewell to the World Cup after group stage matches against the winner Brazil, the USSR and England. Because of the high travel costs they did not enter qualification for the 1962 edition. As though in defiance, Karl Decker's team went on a winning streak in 1960 and 1961 with victories against Scotland, the USSR, Spain, Italy, England and Hungary – the first win in Budapest for 29 years. A temporary high, no more. Then frustration reigned for more than a decade. Highlights such as the historic 3-2 win of a *Baby-Team* with an average age of 23 at Wembley on 20 October 1965 against England (who then went 19 games unbeaten and were world champions the following year) were the exception rather than the rule. Only in the mid-seventies was there a sense of reawakening. Some seasoned legionnaires from the German Bundesliga, such as Hickersberger, Hattenberger and Jara, and Belgium (Krieger), plus a superb goalkeeper (Friedl Koncilia) and exceptional homegrown talents like Pezzey, Prohaska, Krankl, Schachner and Obermayer made up a constellation that promised success.

And the twenty years of waiting for World Cup participation were promptly followed with a bang. 2-1 against Spain, 1-0 against Sweden – after only two matches Austria were through. And after three defeats (1-0 against Brazil, 5-1 against the Netherlands and 1-0 against Italy) West Germany were also vanquished by Helmut Senekowitsch's team; the 3-2 victory with two goals from Hans Krankl being enough to send the reigning world champions home and ending Helmut Schön's career with a failure. The end of the German complex. 5000 fans at the airport in Schwechat when the heroes returned two days after the match in Cordoba. A seventh-place finish at a World Cup has not been repeated yet.

Four years later in Spain, another duel with West Germany made the headlines, but only negative ones. 50,000 fans in Vienna at the team's departure had underlined the high expectations, but with the 1-0 against the neighbours in Gijon the mood changed completely. After half an hour, the playing of football ceased. Since both teams went through with the result, the match turned into an orgy of passes in midfield. The hoped-for national day of celebration turned into a day of infamy. The 44,000 spectators whistled angrily, waved white handkerchiefs as at weak bull fights; Algerian fans held up banknotes to signify bribery and connivance. Outside of the ground, rocks, tomatoes and bananas were thrown at the team buses. The second round provided no grounds for celebration either – a 1-0

defeat to France, a 2-2 draw against Northern Ireland, a flight home. Back in Austria the people were furious. Fans abused the players' families. The hero of Cordoba, Krankl, who hadn't played against Northern Ireland, became the bogeyman and was booed all over Austria (except at Rapid's home matches) for some time. He still says now, "If the Germans around Paul Breitner, Stielike or Karl-Heinz Rummenigge in Gijon had had any idea how bad and tired we really were, a terrible debacle would have been inevitable for us."

Of those who had played in Spain, Herbert Prohaska remained to help qualify for the World Cup in Italy in 1990 in three games in the last year of his playing career, but the headlines were made by younger men. In particular there was Toni Polster, seven years after his debut, scoring all three goals in the decisive 3-0 win over East Germany two weeks after the fall of the Berlin Wall. Dreams of the World Cup were already flourishing after friendlies against Argentina (with Diego Maradona) and the Netherlands, but the awakening was bitter. 1-0 defeats to Italy and Czechoslovakia and a 2-1 win against the United States were not enough to progress. 20,000 red-white-red fans in Florence were devastated. But what happened two and a half months later, on 12 September 1990, made Austria the laughing stock of the entire football world. In the European Championship qualifiers they played the Faroe Islands in their first ever competitive match. Because the amateurs from the sheep islands had no grass pitch, they had to divert to Landskrona in Sweden. The goalkeeper Jens Martin Knudsen, in a white bobble hat, held firmly onto the "nil". The coach Josef Hickersberger had told the players that if they played badly they'd just about win; if they played well they'd win by eight goals. The day after the disaster he resigned. The entire qualification campaign was a disappointment – but then came a new boss and with him new hope: Ernst Happel, now an internationally successful coach, took over in 1992 with the words, "Ok, so, we're going to qualify." It was a suicide mission, but that did not deter him. When he accepted the job offer from the federation president Beppo Mauhart, he said laconically, "Well then, let's have a revolution." It only lasted 11 months. Happel was terminally ill, passed away at the Innsbruck university hospital on November 14. Just before, he dictated a last message to his life partner Veronika: "I've left behind a squad that can be the basis for more development. They just have to do something with it, they have to believe in it. They have to be proud of the national team, have to have an emotional connection, otherwise it won't work. It was a wonderful year. You'll see, something will come of it. Tell everyone that." His successor Herbert Prohaska, appointed as Under-21 coach by Happel, couldn't manage it for either the 1994 World Cup or Euro 1996, only for the 1998 World Cup in France. Convincing in qualifying, finishing with six wins in a row and in first place ahead of Sweden and Scotland. Again, a similar constellation as in 1978: good legionaries from strong leagues, good goalkeepers, internationally competitive players from the domestic league. But, unlike in 1978, no exceptional talents.

Two 1-1 draws against Cameroon and Chile, both times with an equaliser in the last minute, then a 2-1 defeat to Italy to finish. That was the last waltz in Paris that denied them progress. They were never the wonder boys that Udo Jürgens sang about in the official Austrian World Cup song. Until Marcel Koller led this Austria side to qualify for Euro 2016, Prohaska was the last Austrian manager under whom they managed to qualify for a major tournament. His 51st match as coach was his last. The 9-0 defeat against Spain in Valencia in qualifying for Euro 2000 was the biggest defeat for Austria since the 11-1 loss against England on 8 June 1908 in Vienna. Prohaska didn't hesitate before resigning: "The coach leaves and the story is done."

All his successors failed. Otto Baric got as far as the play-off of the World Cup qualifiers for 2002, Hans Krankl managed neither Euro 2004 nor the World Cup 2006; as hosts for Euro 2008 they also reached no heights. One point from three games, then Josef Hickersberger left for the second time. The Czech veteran Karel Brückner took over, left after eight months because he saw no hope for the future. Didi Constantini radically reorganised and rejuvenated but had to leave when, after the 2010 World Cup, Euro 2012 was also missed. His successor surprised – nobody had expected the former Swiss midfielder Koller. In the three and a half years under his command Austria climbed from 85th in the world rankings to the top 20, despite missing out on qualification to the 2014 World Cup in Brazil. He is now Austria's favourite Swiss. In the first six qualifiers they lost none, won five, three of them away, a victory in Moscow for the first time since 1961. Now the motto is France, we'll be back! After a break of 17 years.

For Prohaska, who witnessed the ups and downs of Austria as player and manager, the current soaring flight is no surprise. Koller is the first Austria manager to select a starting XI, plus several substitutes, who all play abroad. None of his predecessors could draw on so many. There is an exceptional player again: the 23-year-old David Alaba of Bayern, to whom Constantini gave his debut at 18, and some who have noticeably improved abroad, especially Dynamo Kyiv's 24-year-old defender Aleksandar Dragovic, who is now being scouted by top European clubs, and the engine of Bremen's midfield, Zlatko Junuzovic. Prohaska says, "We are now seeing the positive results of a youth program that was initiated ten years ago with academies that keep delivering strong players. Of all the team legionnaires, only three went abroad as youth players: the others got their training in Austria. So it can't be so bad." And that's why Prohaska is convinced that the soaring flight won't just be temporary this time around: "Something is being made for years to come. It's not a coincidence that Austria's youth teams have recently qualified more and more often for World Cups and European competitions." Of the team that came fourth at the U20 World Cup in Canada seven years ago, six players are in Koller's core squad. Prohaska says, looking back: "Now the association has enough money to invest in the next generations. That was missing in 1978. At that time we weren't just being paid in money but also in VCRs and TVs."

Koller no longer finds the typical Viennese grumbling annoying: he understands and respects its nature. Prohaska doesn't deny his achievements. "It doesn't do him any favours to be feted as the messiah. He doesn't want that either, he keeps a low profile. What was crucial was that he built a squad that he stuck with. No matter what happened to the players at their clubs. I admit, I wouldn't have had that courage." The success proves Koller right. The goalkeeper Robert Almer has made more appearances under Koller than for his three German teams – Fortuna Düsseldorf, Cottbus and Hannover – put together. He kept his faith in Marc Janko when he was sidelined by Trabzonspor and trained alone for months. When he attempted a new start at FC Sydney, Koller flew him in without a second thought. Janko thanked him with goals, managed to return to Europe aged 32, signed for FC Basel, the champion of Koller's native Switzerland, and just before opened the door to France with his 21st goal for his country, an attractive overhead kick for the victory in Moscow. In Austria nobody now doubts him or even Koller.

After this, the players set themselves the goal of finishing the qualifying campaign unbeaten. The last time this had happened was in 1977. They achieved their self-imposed task, impressing particularly in a 4-1 win over Sweden at the Friends Arena in Stockholm, where they had failed to secure a ticket to the World Cup in Brazil two years earlier.

Even Zlatan Ibrahimović congratulated them: "You were the better team!" At 4 o'clock in the morning hundreds of fans were still waiting at the airport in Vienna for the return of the heroes of Stockholm. As a bonus it was followed with a 3-2 win in Podgorica against Montenegro, a 3-0 win against

Liechtenstein at the Happel-Stadion – sold out on a Monday night. And with that Austria were in the top ten of the Fifa world rankings for the first time. Koller's reign began in 77th place.

In Austria nobody now doubts Koller. One thing has never changed in the soul of Austrian football: there is only ever jubilation or desolation. Nothing in between. Right now the hype around the team is greater than it has been for decades. At the end of June, 3% of the population said they believed Austria would be European champions in France in 2016; it has already risen since then.

156

Fiction

"Surely you're good enough to
do that?"

Quantum of Bobby

Can Bobby stop David Beckham getting sent off at the 1998 World Cup?

By Iain Macintosh

Theorising that radio controlled clouds could help Qatar manufacture a climate suitable for football, the authorities experimented... and nearly killed their national coach Bobby Manager with one. Manager awoke to find himself trapped in the past, facing challenges that were not his own, driven to change history for the better. His only guide on this journey is Karren Brady, or at least a subconscious manifestation of Karren Brady, who speaks to him in a voice that only Bobby can hear. And so Bobby Manager finds himself leaping from life to life, striving to put right what once went wrong and hoping each time that is next leap will be the leap home.

Darkness. And yet... not darkness. Darkness only indicates the absence of light. This was an altogether more complete affair. An absence of everything. Of light, of time, of space. Of everything. Like a blank canvas, but without the canvas. And the easel. And whatever it was you were intending to paint. And indeed the very concept of painting. It was still and it was silent and it was nothing.

There was a polite cough. And then a man's voice.

"Erm... excuse me?"

Nothing.

"Karren?"

Nothing.

"Karren... I've been here for a very long time. Are you... erm... are you planning to send me anywhere, or is that it? Do we just fade out?"

Nothing.

"...am I dead?"

Nothing.

"Oh God, that's it, isn't it? I'm dead. The cloud killed me. I've been wiped out by a fucking cloud. That's... that's the most ridiculous celebrity death since Rod Hull lost the signal to the Manchester United game. Oh God, I'm actually dead!"

A woman's voice.

"Calm down, Bobby. You're not dead yet."

"Karren! Where have you been?"

"I've been tied up with a good book, I'm afraid. Simply haven't had the time."

"A book?! You left me in this sensory

abyss for months for a book?"

"In my defence, it was a very good book. You'd like it."

"I couldn't give a toss if it was *War and bloody Peace*! Let me out of here!"

A sigh.

"Fine. Hold on."

There was a swirling noise and then the feeling that my soul was being hauled out of my body by a giant sink plunger. My lungs were pulled against my ribs, my brain to the front of my skull. There was blinding light from all directions, burning, coruscating light. And then a thud that took the wind out of me. And the taste of grass in my mouth.

"Hang on, lads," shouted a voice. "That looks a nasty one. You okay, Bobby?"

"Urgh," I said. This never got any easier. I lifted my head up and rolled onto my side.

"Sorry, Bobby!" said Rob Lee, leaning over me. "I didn't see you there. Are you okay?"

"Urgh," I said again. "Head."

"Get back out there, Rob," said a voice. "I've got this. But remember; just another ten minutes. You are the keeper of your own destiny, if you like. But I don't want you getting sunburned." Big hands reached underneath my shoulders and hauled me to my feet. "Come on, Bobby. Let's see what the damage is."

"Glenn Hoddle?" I said, looking at him, resplendent in his England tracksuit.

"Oh dear," he said. "Could be a bit of concussion. That's all we need right now. Get yourself back into the changing rooms. Doctor Crane is in there with Gareth. We can't lose you both on the same day. Go see the doc and then come with me to see Eileen. She'll sort you out."

"Okay," I said groggily. "Okay, I know how this goes." I turned away and left them to it, trudging towards the changing rooms on the edge of the pitch. And then a loud shout made me turn back.

"NO, NO, NO! How many times do I have to tell you, David?" shouted Glenn as he stomped across the pitch. "Not like that. Come on, it's not difficult. You tee the ball up to yourself, catch it on the toes of your right foot, lift it over your own head while you turn a full 360 degrees, catch it on the inside of your left foot, hold the ball perfectly motionless, then hop twice, flick it up and wallop it with your right. Surely you're good enough to do that?"

David Beckham stood forlornly on the pitch, hands on hips, head sagging.

"This is nice," said Karren, from deep inside my head. "The south of France. The beginning of the summer. A nation's hopes in the balance. A sweet and vulnerable David Beckham who needs to be looked after. I'm grown to cherish these moments, Bobby."

"I'm glad one of us is enjoying this, Karren," I said. "Personally, I'd rather just be back in the real world, managing a real football team."

"You *are* in the real world, Bobby," said Karren pointedly. "It's just that you're a pallid pile of flesh in a surgical gown that wouldn't survive more than 30 seconds if there was a power cut."

"You could just try to be nice, Karren. It really wouldn't be that hard."

"Precisely," she snapped. "It wouldn't be hard at all. It would be easy. So easy, in fact, that you could put your few remaining operational synapses on standby and glide through what little remained of your life before total shutdown. Would you like that? Or would you like me to continue pushing you and testing you in the futile hope that your mental pilot light ignites and you can go home?"

"Fine," I groaned. "Carry on."

"Thank you."

"So, what have we got? It's 1998, I've got that much. It's the England training camp and Glenn Hoddle is the manager. They're going to play three group games and then get knocked by Argentina on penalties."

"Almost right," said Karren. "They've already beaten Tunisia. They have Romania and Colombia left to play before, assuming that you don't knock them off their stride and make things worse, Argentina in the second round."

"The game they lost on penalties. So what do I do? You said when we went back to 1990 that some things were too powerful to be changed and that England getting knocked out on penalties was one of them. What's the mission?"
"You have to figure that out for yourself, Bobby. Maybe you should ask yourself how England could possibly avoid going

to a penalty shoot-out with Argentina?"

There was more commotion on the training pitch.

"NO, DAVID! I don't want you to just cut inside and play the simple ball. I want you to land the ball on his instep from a range of 65 yards without breaking stride. Surely you're good enough to do that?"

David Beckham stood silently, but his eyes were ablaze with a thousand fires.

"Ah," I said. "I think I might know where to focus my efforts. Beckham was sent off, wasn't he? Dismissed for a moment of furious petulance, lashing out at Diego Simeone. England were forced to play out the rest of the game with 10 men. They nearly did it too. I think I can handle this one, Karren."

Back in the dressing room, I sat down quietly and watched Dr Crane work on Gareth Southgate's ankle. It didn't look good.

"You might be all right, Gareth," he said. "But we won't know until the morning. Chin up, son. At least it's not broken. Now then, Bobby. Let's have a look at this head. Don't want you missing out either. The gaffer needs everyone fit for Romania, he's been fretting about it again. Says he's had one of his dreams."

"One of his dreams?" I asked as he shone a bright light into my eye.

"Ah, you know how he gets. He reads a lot into his dreams. I try to tell him that it's just his subconscious fighting with his digestive system, but he does like to consider that they might be premonitions. I hope he's right. I had a dream that I slipped one to Ginger Spice last night. Ha ha!"

"Mmmm," I mused. "Speaking of which, how do you think him and David Beckham are getting along?"

Dr Crane sucked air through his teeth like a mechanic presented with a mysterious and soon-to-be profitable oil leak.

"Well, that is a thing indeed, yes. David was very put out not to be included against Tunisia and he wasn't happy about being paraded in front of the press afterwards either." He leaned forward conspiratorially. "And as you know, Bobby, he's not going to be playing against Romania either. I thin-" The door opened and he fell silent.

"How are they, Doc?" asked Glenn.

"Well," said Dr Crane. "Gareth has some nasty bruising, so he's touch and go for Romania, but he should recover soon. There's no major ligament damage."

"Right," said Glenn. "I'll tell the press he's in a medically induced coma and that his family are saying farewell. "

"What?!" spluttered Dr Crane.

"Got to keep them guessing, Doc. Haven't you read Sun Tzu? All warfare is based on deception. Get his wife over here and tip off the photographers. See if you can make her cry in the taxi, make it look good. Now, what about Bobby?"

"Erm... nothing more than a bang on the head. No sign of concussion, but best for him to take it easy for a couple of days. Bobby, if you get any headaches or dizziness, you come find me immediately, eh?"

"Thanks, Doc," I said.

"Walk with me, Bobby," said Glenn. "We have much to discuss, if you like."

We left the changing room and strolled back to the hotel complex. You had to hand it to Glenn, he'd found us a lovely place to make camp in France. Neat lawns, clean buildings and absolute solitude. It was perfect. We even passed a huge games room filled with pool tables and arcade machines. The players, their training complete, sauntered around in flip-flops. We walked past and stepped into a smaller room on the side, with comfy chairs and piles of leather-bound books.

"Here again, Graeme?" smiled Glenn. "You and your books, you big book-head."

Graeme Le Saux sighed.

"It's just a Tom Clancy," he said. "It's actually really good, it's all about submarines and politics."

"Yeah, yeah, listen; can you give us the room?" Graeme nodded and went to put the book back. "You can take the book with you."

"Not a bloody chance," said Graeme grimly. "They'll only try to flush it down the toilet again." He carefully hid it behind a cushion and left the room, pausing only to let a small middle-aged woman through the door first. "Eileen!" beamed Glenn.

"Glenn, ya lovely little bastard! 'Ow are ya?" "Bobby, I want you to spend some time with Eileen. I know that you've always been a little dubious about this sort of thing, but I think it can really help. Especially after your bang on the head."

"Ooooh, 'as he 'ad a bang on the noggin?" giggled Eileen. "I'll soon set that right, donchoo worry."

"Come on, Bobby," said Glenn kindly. "Relax into it. I was a sceptic once, you know. But then Eileen laid her hands on me and I could see that it was my preconceptions that were holding me back. I'd created a prison of my own ignorance, if you like, but she was able to throw a rope ladder over the perimeter fence and help me to freedom."

Eileen stepped forwards, her hands outstretched. I wasn't so sure.

"It's OK, Glenn," I said. "Seriously. It's just a bit of a knock. I'll take a couple of paracetamol with a glass of water and I'll be fine."

"Bobby," said Glenn, placing his hand on mine. "Do this for me. As a favour."

Eileen moved around behind me and lowered me into my seat.

"Don't you worry about a fing, Bob," she said. "I've laid my healin' hands on 'undreds of troubled noggins and the only bloke to complain was that tousle-haired ginger nugget that Glenn don't pick no more. You'll be fine, my sweetheart."

I sighed and sat down in the seat. I felt her fingers curl into my hair and across my scalp.

"Mmmm," she murmured. "I can feel the troubles already, Bob. You should've been to... oh."

Her fingers tensed on my head for a moment.

"Everything all right up there?" I asked.

"Oh Bob..." she said quietly.

"Eileen?" said Glenn. "You've gone as white as a sheet, what's wrong?"

"Oh...." she said in a small voice. "So many lives. So many short, short lives. And something else. SomeONE else."

"I told you she was good," said Glenn with a broad grin on his face.

"No..." said Eileen. "No, I won't leave! Who are you? WHO ARE YOU?"

"Eileen?" said Glenn.

"What's going on up there?" I said, trying in vain to turn my head against her steely grip. "And what's that smell?"

"So much malevolence!" wailed Eileen. "Her eyes! She is terrible!" Her grip slackened off and she fell away.

"EILEEN!" cried Glenn and he jumped forward to catch her as she crumpled to the floor. There was a stench in the air, like rotten eggs left in the sunshine. I reached up and felt my head. My hair was singed and crunched in my fingers like dry grass.

The door crashed open. Martin Keown and David Batty ran in with pool cues in their hands. Behind them still more players craned in to see what was going on.

"What's happening boss? What's wrong with Mrs Drewery? Why is there smoke rising from Bobby's head?" said Keown.

"She's had a funny turn, Martin," said Glenn, kneeling over her. "Get her a glass of water, will you?"

"She will come for it," groaned Eileen groggily. "She will come for it. She will come for the people's arena where the river meets the road. She cannot be stopped. She cannot... be... stopped." Eileen's eyes rolled back in her head and she fell silent.

"What an interesting woman," said Karren quietly. "Weak, but interesting."

Eileen wouldn't come near me after that. Every time she saw me in the hotel, she'd let out a little squeal and rush off in the opposite direction. But we had bigger problems than a traumatised faith healer. Romania beat us 2-1 in the second group-stage game and our survival was at stake. Everything came down to the last match against Colombia.

"I don't know what went wrong, lads." said Glenn over coffee at our coaches meeting the next morning.

"I don't know either, Mr Grimsdale!" gurned Peter Taylor.

Glenn stared at him.

"You've been warned about this, Peter."

"Sorry, boss."

"It's just one of those things, Glenn," I said comfortingly. "It wasn't a bad game, it was just a couple of mistakes and they both got punished. There's no need to do anything dramatic. And look on the bright side. Young Michael Owen scored and David Beckham looked very comfortable in midfield. There's a lot of promise in this team and there's every chance that they'll grow in strength as the tournament continues."

Glenn looked up.

"I think we need more M People," he said. "We're searching for the hero inside ourselves, if you like, when we should be moving on up. And if we're going to have our one night in heaven then it'll certainly be a sight for sore eyes."

"I don't think that's the solution, Glenn," I said.

"Okay, it's settled," he said, standing up. "More M People. Thanks for coming, lads. I always welcome these little chats."

After training that day, I took David aside for a talk.

"You're okay, David. You're doing well. You were great when you came on the other night and I've got a feeling that the boss is going to pick you against Colombia."

David shook his head sadly.

"He hates me," he said. "He's always making me look silly in training. He does his fancy free-kicks and then shouts when I can't do them as well as him! I do my own free-kicks, they're good free-kicks too!"

"They're great free-kicks, David. You keep doing them. Especially if you happen to get one against Colombia, OK? Promise me that. The boss just has his ways. He's trying to keep your feet on the ground because he's worried that the bewitching lure of celebrity is going to corrupt you."

David looked at me with anger in his eyes. "That will NEVER happen! Why does everyone think that celebrity will change me? Elton John said the same thing to me when we was on Tom Jones's yacht last summer. It makes me so angry."

"Look, David," I said. "The most important thing is that you keep your head. You can't afford to get angry and, you know, lash out. The next time you get angry, why don't you just shut your eyes and count to ten?"

"Well, that ain't gonna work," said David. "How am I supposed to see me fingers with me eyes shut?"

"Okay," I conceded the point. "Maybe just keep your eyes open."

He may not have seen the significance of my counting advice, but David certainly didn't forget what I said about his free-kicks. He whipped one home in the first half to double the lead after Darren Anderton had smashed in the opener from a narrow angle.

"Not bad at all, David," said Glenn afterwards. "I would have played a simple one-two from the dead ball, flipped up the return and put a bit of spin on the eventual finish, if you like, but your way wasn't bad either."

It was progress of sorts.

It's funny, really. You would think that

having seen the Argentina game already would make it less stressful, but that wasn't the case at all. Argentina's penalty after six minutes, England's penalty after ten minutes. Michael Owen's astonishing goal to put England in front. Javier Zanetti putting the finishing touch to a perfectly-worked free-kick just before the break. It was tense, nerve-racking stuff.

"Let's just get them in and calm them down," said Glenn as the half-time whistle blew. "I've got just the solution." And with that, he sprinted down the tunnel and into the dressing room.

"Well done, lads," I said as I stood by the door, patting them on the head. "Great goal, Michael. Keep at it, Alan." They all trooped in and sat down on the benches as Dr Crane handed out energy drinks. Then all the lights went off and Glenn emerged from the shower room with a tray of lit aromatherapy candles.

"Peter," he said quietly. "Hit the vibes."

Peter Taylor pointed a remote control at the stereo in the corner of the room and the sound of a gently teased saxophone filled the room.

"Everyone take a candle," said Glenn. "And just let the sound of Kenny G take you over. It's from his Billboard chart-topping album _The Moment_ and this is your moment, if you like."

The players exchanged looks, but after a shrug and a nod from Alan Shearer, they began to hand the candles out among themselves. But David Beckham wouldn't take one.

"Are you all right, David?" I asked him as

G's understated brass tones built to a thoroughly unsatisfying crescendo.

Veins were standing out on David's head as he sat shuddering in the corner. He was digging his finger nails into the tops of his thighs, leaving marks in the skin.

"I... can't... stand... Kenny... fucking... G..." he grimaced.

"Just try to relax," I said. "It'll be over soon."

David breathed heavily through his mouth like a man trying not to vomit on a rollercoaster.

"I... am... so.... angry."

"Relax, David." I said. "Just try to count to 10, like I said."

He turned to look at me, his eyes wide in the gloom.

"It's dark, Bobby. How can I be sure that I'll get it right?"

I had to stop the madness. I stepped over to Glenn and gave him a nudge.

"Boss? Don't you think this is a bit much? Shouldn't we just try to focus on the game? Maybe go over that free-kick and how to avoid it happening again?"

"No, Bobby. Kenny G really works. His soothing sounds settle even the greatest rage."

"Hmmm," I said. "Didn't Paul Gascoigne smash seven shades of shit out of your hotel room when you put Kenny G on?"

"I'm not at home to negativity right now," said Glenn. "Take a candle and sit down."

I was so worried about the second half. And rightly so. Perhaps Argentina had sensed that David wasn't quite right, that he could be targeted. They went for him straight from the whistle. The ball fell to him in the centre-circle, loose, in need of taming. For a moment, Beckham had it, moving into it, bringing it under control, shielding it with his body. And then a flash of dark blue and a heavy thump. Like an unmarked police car going through crates of watermelons in a 70s cop movie, Diego Simeone crashed into Beckham, knocking him flat on his face.

"Come on, David," I hissed. "Hold it together. Hold it together."

He lay still, his leg twitched for a moment, but then he relaxed. Referee Kim Milton Nielsen strode over, reached for his pocket and showed a yellow card to Simeone. The Argentine midfielder held his hands outstretched in front of him as if to say, "Who? Me?" Nielsen nodded and scribbled his name down.

"Yes!" I shouted. "Well done, David! Well done, son!"

Glenn turned and shot me a look.

"Well done? For getting fouled?"

"He didn't react though, did he? That's the thing. That's the important bit."

"Why would he react?" Glenn chuckled. "You're an odd one, Bobby."

Simeone shrugged at Nielsen and then

stepped over to David, leaned towards him and whispered something in his ear. David pulled back, his face contorted with rage. And then he nutted him. There was a horrible crunching noise and Simeone fell to his knees trying to hold what remained of his nose onto his face. The Argentina players howled in rage, their bench rose as one and ran onto the pitch. It was chaos, people were pushing each other over, fists were raised, the crowd roared in fury.

Glenn just stood there, shaking his head sadly. He spat on the ground.

"I knew I should have handed out the life-force crystals as well," he groaned. "Damn your impatience, Glenn Hoddle. Damn you."

David slipped away from the melee, walking away with his eyes fixed on the tunnel. I left the bench and ran to him.

"David! What on earth were you thinking?!"

He looked at me. Tears wobbling in his eyes.

"Why does everyone say *that* about her?

Why is everyone so obsessed? We did it that way ONCE and we didn't even like it! It's so unfair!"

I reached out a hand, but I seemed to pass right through him. The stadium around me, the supporters, the noise, it all began to melt.

"Karren!" I shouted.

"I'm sorry, Bobby. But it's not just unsuccessful England penalty shoot-outs that cannot be changed. England must always have a scapegoat too. There must always be someone whose one moment of shame can be used to obscure widespread failings brought on by arrogance and insularity. You cannot fight nature. You were never meant to succeed here. You were only meant to try."

"I just want to go home, Karren! I just want to go home!"

I fell, first into the grass and then down through the soil and into the earth, spinning viciously as I went. I was leaping. I was leaping through time and space. I hoped against hope that this leap would be my leap home. Oh boy, was I wrong. Ⓑ

166

Greatest Games

"Nobody in Yugoslavia would forget
where they were at that moment."

Hajduk Split v Crvena Zvezda (abandoned)

Yugoslav First League, Stadion Poljud, Split, 4 May 1980

By Charles Ducksbury

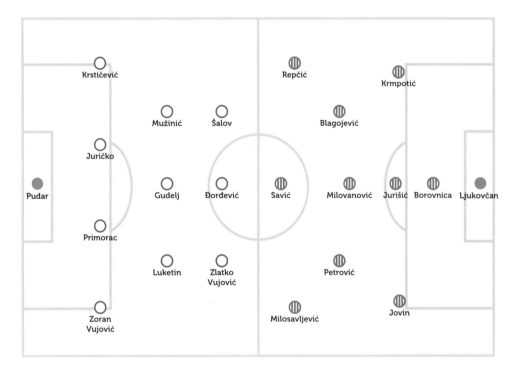

It was impossible to avoid news of Josip Broz Tito's deteriorating health as the heat of summer descended on Yugoslavia in May 1980. Daily updates from the president's medical team were presented via TV, radio and in print format. Aged 87 and confined to Ljubljana's Medical Centre, he had already had his leg amputated and, despite the efforts of his team

to reassure his citizens, it was clear that the nation's leader was days from departing. Yugoslavs tried to carry on their duties as normal, but the country was preparing for the end of an era and the beginning of a new one that everybody knew might be difficult.

Ivica Profaca, a 15 year old from Split, enjoyed a familiar pre-match ritual. He would meet his friends from school and his local neighbourhood a few hours before kick-off, before then heading to the stadium, past the stalls selling seeds and nuts, to grab their usual spot in the stands. On 4 May 1980, Profaca made his usual trip with a quicker pace, as many do before the big games.

Hajduk Split were hosting the league leaders Crvena Zvezda in the Yugoslav First League. Hajduk had won the championship the previous season and sat two points behind Zvezda with nine games to go. The Croatians had already won 1-0 in Belgrade earlier in the season and were expected to win again this time; Hajduk were the only team who held a positive record against Zvezda when Yugoslavia fragmented in 1991, winning 35 matches to Zvezda's 32. As if history and the notorious atmosphere Hajduk fans created weren't enough, the Serbians were heading to Split on the back of a 2-0 loss at relegation-threatened Budućnost.

The 1979-80 season had been one of change for Hajduk. They had left their historical Stadion Stari Plac – the Plinara – earlier in the season to move to the city's new Gradski Stadion u Poljudu – known simply as Poljud – built for the 1979 Mediterranean Games. Tito had opened the new stadium and the Hajduk captain Dražen Mužinić led a delegation of players to meet their leader. "He spoke to us like we were family," he said. "We were supposed to meet him for ten minutes but after 45 minutes we were still talking, and it was clear he was a big fan of Hajduk."

With an increased capacity of 55,000, up from Plinara's 20,000, more fans could watch games, but many felt the atmosphere generated by the tight old ground had been lost. Soon after moving into the new ground, they played one of Hajduk's most famous games, as 52,000 witnessed a 3-2 victory over Kevin Keegan's Hamburg in the European Cup quarter-finals. The Croatians had lost 1-0 in Germany so crashed out on away goals, but those present claim it was one of Hajduk's most complete performances[1].

Ivica wasn't really aware of politics, but he had picked up his parents' concerns about Tito and much of the conversation in the town focused on the president. Tito officially ruled Yugoslavia for 35 years from the end of the Second World War. His life is a story of near-death, politics and a firmness, or even harshness, that held the country together throughout his reign, a country on the brink of break-up prior to his leadership.

Born in 1892 as the seventh of fifteen children to a Croatian father and a Slovenian mother, Josip Broz lived a peasant life in the small farming village of Kumrovec, close to Zagreb. He was employed first as a locksmith, then as a mechanic before leaving to work in Austria and Germany. It was in Vienna that he first entered politics, becoming a member of the Social Democrats in 1910. He was drafted to fight for the Austro-Hungarian army in World War I, being captured by the Russians, although he did then join the Red Army following the Russian Revolution of 1917. He spent

---

[1] *See Aleksandar Holiga's piece in* The Blizzard *Issue Ten.*

much of his time between 1915 and 1920 and a great deal of the 1930s in Moscow, but there is little evidence of exactly *what* he was doing. A document recently released by the US National Security Agency entitled "Is Yugoslav President Tito Really a Yugoslav?" concluded, through analysing Tito's speech patterns and grammar, that his accent was less Croatian and more Russian or Polish – although it's far more probable he just spoke with the characteristic thick accent of his region, interspersed with some Slovenian, Russian and Serbian terms. One popular urban myth was that Tito died in Russian captivity in 1915, his replacement hand-picked by the Soviets. His sympathisers, however, simply put it down to the amount of time he spent in Russia, even if the whispers never truly went away.

His return to Croatia saw him sign up as a member of the banned Communist Party of Yugoslavia (KPJ, something that brought eventual arrest). After release and spending much time in the Soviet Union, he was eventually appointed leader of the KPJ in 1937 following Stalin's purges of the party's leadership, although it is said it was Stalin himself who sent Tito to reinvigorate the party and attach Yugoslavia to the Eastern Bloc.

After the Axis powers, lead by Italy and Germany, had occupied Yugoslavia and forced the Royal Yugoslav Army to surrender during the Second World War, Tito founded his Partisan guerrilla force in 1941 to fight not only against the Axis powers, but also the Chetniks, led by Draža Mihailović. They began as a Royalist resistance movement but became more concerned with battling Partisans and the ethnic cleansing of the non-Serb population, even collaborating wth the Axis forces in some areas. That eventually led the Allies to switch their support from the Chetniks to the Partisans, even though they were predominantly Communist.

The Partisans are a divisive topic. Some Yugoslavs were proud of a group that stood up to Nazi occupation, liberating large pockets of land from Nazi control, but others point to the killing of tens of thousands of members of rival military groups, such as the Croatian-nationalist Ustaše and the Chetniks, who worked with with the Axis powers, as well as civilians who were perceived as collaborators. Mihailović himself – although very controversially rehabilitated in Serbia this year – was tried and executed for high treason and war crimes, as the supreme commander of a military group that not only fought Partisans, but also collaborated with the Axis powers, for which there is plenty of evidence.

Tito assumed the role of prime minister in 1945 and sought to cleanse Yugoslavia of political opponents. In 1948, Yugoslavia was ejected from the Communist Bloc by Stalin after Tito defied Soviet financial and political demands. Threats of an economic blockade and military intervention only solidified Tito's popularity amongst Yugoslavs, who were delighted to have a leader fighting for their rights rather than submitting to the eastern superpower as other communist nations had. By 1953 Tito was named the first president of Yugoslavia, before the 1963 constitution declared him president for life.

The level of repression declined as time went by; his enemies had long been vanquished and those born in post-War Yugoslavia accepted their way of life. Tito attempted to steer a middle path between east and west, sought to maintain good relations with Arab nations as part of his commitment to the non-Aligned movement and was a staunch supporter of the UN.

Football under Tito started again soon after the war, but only after most clubs were disbanded for alleged collaboration with the enemy, including the Zagreb sides Građanski and Concordia, and Belgrade club SK Jugoslavija, all of them pre-war champions. In their place came the clubs of today, including Crvena Zvezda and Dinamo Zagreb, but Hajduk were the only pre-war champion not be disbanded due to their role in the war. Hajduk were invited to play in Italy's Serie A after the city of Split was occupied by Italian forces, being offered flights to all away games if they changed their name to the Italianised AC Spalato. Hajduk declined, choosing instead to disband voluntarily. The Italian fascists started their own club, but couldn't force any former Hajduk players to sign up, with many members preferring to join the Communist resistance.

Hajduk were reformed and used as the team of the resistance, sent them abroad to promote Yugoslavia (although there's no evidence Tito, who had little interest in football, bore any responsibility for the scheme). They played several games against teams of servicemen in Italy, most famously losing to a team of young professionals including Stan Cullis and Tom Finney 7-2 in front of 40,000 in Bari in 1944, before winning the rematch (against a weaker side) 1-0 in liberated Split later that year. They also played

friendlies in Egypt, Palestine and Syria. Tito even met Hajduk's players three times, leading to the story that Hajduk were his team. After the war ended, Hajduk were invited to move to Belgrade to become the team of the Yugoslav army. The club refused, which in turn gave birth to Partizan Belgrade, formed later that year.

On that fateful day in 1980, Profaca, wearing white as almost all the fans did, and still do when attending Poljud to see Hajduk, took his place in the north stand. His spot was near the front, towards the west stand, with the real tough guys standing in the centre directly behind the goal, a new home after gathering in the east stand at the old Plinara Stadion.

Despite levels of violence being relatively low during Tito's reign, there were still instances of fighting and brawling at football matches. Torcida Split are thought to be the oldest supporters group in Europe, having been formed in 1950 by a group of students prior to a Hajduk-Zvezda game. Wanting to encourage their side by waving flags and banners, they were soon investigated by the Communist party who were concerned by gatherings of unruly young men and quickly banned the name. One of the founders of Torcida, Vjenceslav Žuvela, was not only excluded from the Communist party but sentenced to three years in prison (later reduced to three months) for wearing a badge with the letter T next to the letter H. Some claim the prosecuting authorities interpreted that as denoting Torcida Hrvatska (Torcida Croatia), although "Hajduk" would be the far more likely meaning and it's more likely that any citizens' association – formal or informal

– not affiliated with the Communist Party was viewed with suspicion.

The gatherings continued but to avoid arrest the meetings were conducted without the Torcida name. In the 1970s Hajduk's youngsters began meeting at bars on the sea front, listening to music and poetry about life as a Hajduk fan in the past. A Torcida fan website notes that the seventies were a time when there were changes in football violence, with a rise in incidents involving supporters of opposition teams.

Because of Hajduk fans' reputation for violence and intimidation, many away supporters didn't attend games in Split and in May 1980 there were hardly any Zvezda supporters inside Poljud. The fixture had brought out the worst in supporters in 1974 when Hajduk fans and soldiers supporting Zvezda clashed, leading to numerous arrests and injuries before the soldiers were evacuated from the stadium. That, though, was an isolated incident involving a few dozen people, long before the ultra movement had developed its edge and its mass following, and for the most part the game was often seen as a celebration of Yugoslavia, the two biggest and best-supported clubs meeting, with large crowds and a high standard of football.

Profaca began chanting and cheering for Hajduk, shouting "Gypsies" at Zvezda's players whenever they touched the ball; to use such an insult in the street would have led to a reprimand or even arrest, but in such a large crowd it was impossible to spot individual culprits.

The game was as tense as was to be expected but, as it turned out, the actual match was of little consequence. No newspapers carried a report of the game and almost all the available video evidence is of the events after the referee stopped the match. The vast majority who were there remember very little of the play, although those who can remember details describe a balanced affair of few chances. Some papers and many subsequent reports stated that the match was 0-0 before the spectacle was brought to a halt in the 43rd minute, at 19:12, but it was in fact 1-1; Vladimir 'Pižon' Petrović had given Zvezda the lead from a penalty he himself won in the 13th minute, before Hajduk equalised as Zoran Vujović swept home from eight yards 15 minutes later.

Edo Pezzi is a retired radio commentator. Now 73, he can still recall vividly the precise details of the events leading up the announcement that Tito had died. Pezzi was squeezed into the press gallery at Poljud, describing events to his listeners when Split's leading politician and president of Hajduk Ante Skataretiko walked into his commentary booth and gestured for him to stop his broadcast immediately, for he had to make an announcement over the loudspeaker.

As Pezzi was being taken off air, Ivica Profaca noticed a club official walk to the edge of the pitch and say something to the referee. The cheering and chanting stopped as both teams were asked to line up in the middle of the pitch. Instantly he and most others around him knew what had happened; nobody in Yugoslavia would forget where they were at that moment.

The sight of Hajduk Split and Zvezda players lined up in the middle of the pitch was the perfect image of Tito's

Yugoslavia. Serbs, Croats and the Bosnian officials, led by referee Husref Muharemagić, stood alongside each other, co-existing.

Taking the stadium microphone, Skataretiko proceeded to announce to the 50,000 crowd that at just past 3 o'clock that afternoon President Tito had passed away and the game would be stopped. At first a hush, an almost impossible silence given the size of the crowd and the magnitude of the news they'd just digested. The Hajduk midfielder Dražen Mužinić recalled, "We just weren't prepared for it, and that moment is forever etched in my memory."

Profaca stood motionless. He heard some screams and then sobbing from people dotted around Poljud. Players from both sides and the referee were soon joining them. Muharemagić remembers, "I stopped the game while the ball was at left-back with Mile Jovin. I looked at the presidential boxes but they were empty and I knew what had happened. It was very emotional, I remember it like it was yesterday."

"Before the match we were told this could happen, because information was circulated that Tito had died," explained Dušan Savić, who was on the bench that evening for Zvezda. "There were screams, someone was crying. I think at that moment the dominant feeling was fear of what might happen tomorrow." Savić also noted, "No matter what it was like back then, it was quiet. You could lie down on a bench in the park and no-one would touch you, unlike nowadays."

Spontaneously, the crowd then began singing one of the many songs dedicated

to Tito. "Comrade Tito, we pledge to you that we won't stray from your path." Players continued to weep, others simply stood motionless. Cameramen and photographers walked away wiping tears from their eyes. "Those who say they weren't crying for Tito are lying," said the Macedonian former Zvezda midfielder Boško Đurovski on the 35th anniversary of the match. "I can remember and I'm not ashamed of my tears for Tito."

Mužinić explained, "Because Hajduk and Zvezda were the two top sides, many of us played international football together for Yugoslavia, so naturally we hugged and cried with our friends."

Two photographs taken in the aftermath symbolise perfectly how a nation was feeling. The first image is of the twin brothers Zoran and Zlatko Vujović, both stars in the Hajduk side, slumped on the turf crying. "My brother Zoran fell to his knees," said Zlatko. "I began crying as my heart sank. We cried with the Zvezda players: Petrović, [Miloš] Šestić, Đurovski... they all found it difficult."

The second is of Zoran still lying on the ground, with the Hajduk coach Tomislav Ivić beside him, standing with his head in his hands. Ivić is a symbol of Hajduk and indeed the city of Split. He won three Yugoslav First League titles with the Dalmatians, while also claiming championships in Greece, Holland, Portugal and Belgium. No other coach has won titles in five different countries. Ivić would leave at the end of the season, pursuing a nomadic career that saw him take charge in 14 different countries. The Split native often wondered aloud whether Hajduk could have conquered Europe and perhaps felt a tinge of guilt that he was the first to leave, followed by players. But that was in the future; his emotion to the news of Tito's death represented a city and a nation crying for their departed leader.

Profaca stood still for what seemed like an age, not sure what to do. Without an order and with the game clearly over, the crowd drifted out to a lingering silence; no-one said a word as they trudged back towards the city centre. The situation in Yugoslavia was tense as rumours circulated of Soviet intervention over debts run up in the seventies. With Tito's passing, serious instability was predicted. Normally after a big game there are people shouting in the streets, the hubbub of fans discussing and arguing, but that night there was only quiet. Profaca walked to the meeting hall where his scout group assembled; inside they held a small commemoration for Tito.

The next day Profaca met his schoolmates again and was told that the price of bus tickets had gone up.

"By how much?" he innocently asked.

"Two rubles [ie, the Soviet currency, as opposed to the dinars used in Yugoslavia]," said his giggling friend. With adults mourning openly in the streets, it was left to the youngsters to find a funny side, in blissful ignorance of the gravity of the situation.

Tito's funeral is widely acknowledged to have been the largest state funeral in history until the Nelson Mandela's in 2013. The president's body was brought back from Ljubljana on his own train to Belgrade before his funeral on May 8. It was attended by leaders from both west

and east; mourners arrived from 123 countries and included four kings, 32 presidents and 22 prime ministers. The Yugoslav news agency Tanjug called it "the summit of mankind." The politicians were there to pay their respects, but also to discuss the potential instability in Yugoslavia, with fears the USSR was ready to step in at any moment. As the Kosovar Albanian politician Mahmut Bakalli put it, "We all cried, but we did not know we were burying Yugoslavia."

History of course tells us that Yugoslavs were right to be apprehensive about a future without Tito, but it was from the inside that the country fell apart. A succession plan was drafted by the president as early as 1974, with more autonomy being given to each republic within Yugoslavia; with this, some have since suggested, the first seeds of independence were planted. The idea was to rotate the presidency on a year-by-year basis with each republic assuming control, but by the time Tito died the plan was seen as unworkable. Firstly, those who were lined up for the president's role, such as Tito's right-hand man Edvard Kardelj, had already died, and many potential successors had been purged in Croatia and Serbia in the mid-seventies for being too nationalistic. The beginnings were there for the bloody wars that devastated the region the following decade.

The abandoned game was replayed 17 days later at a packed Poljud. After the 'Derby of Sadness' (as the Yugoslav magazine *Tempo* christened it), Hajduk's season had fallen apart, as they lost 1-0 to Dinamo Zagreb before going down 3-1 to the Montenegrin side Budućnost 3-1. Zvezda drew with Radnički before beating Dinamo 2-1 in Belgrade. The players lined up for kick-off before Ante Skataretiko again took the microphone to ask for a moment's silence to remember Tito. Unlike today there was no gathering in a circle, the players simply stood in their on-field positions and bowed their heads. Zvezda dominated the game, the Bosnian Srebrenko Repčić firing wide when one-on-one and hitting the post via Dušan Savić inside the first ten minutes. Savić eventually found the net, poking home a Petrović free-kick just before the half hour.

Petrović then headed into an empty goal and although Hajduk pulling one back through a Damir Maričić penalty, Savić wrapped up the game in the final minute. Hajduk were out of the title race, seven points behind Zvezda with seven games to play, and dropped as low as fifth after losing their next two games 3-2 to Radnički and then 1-0 at Vardar of Macedonia. After falling to Hamburg and then meekly surrendering their title, Ivić's grand finale was as anti-climatic as his reign was spectacular, eventually finishing ten points behind their Belgrade rivals.

Tito's death allowed the aggressive nationalism that had begun to simmer after 1974 to boil over. Over the following decade Serbia, then Slovenia and Croatia began agitating for greater autonomy and independence, demands that came to a bloody head at the beginning of the 1990s. Zvezda's European Cup win of 1991 was the crowning glory of Yugoslav football and the final act of a sporting nation, a team of Serbians, Croatians, Bosnians, Montenegrins and Macedonians beating Marseille on penalties in Bari. But the break-up of Yugoslavia was by then inevitable, and with it the disintegration of its greatest side. It's highly unlikely a team from the former Yugoslavia will ever come even remotely close to repeating that success, even less so with the domestic make-up of that Zvezda team. Tito's death not only buried Yugoslavia, but also Yugoslavian football. Ⓑ

175

Eight Bells

"He was always a great
penalty saver, even in training,"

One-Hit Wonders

A selection of players who enjoyed a fleeting moment of fame

By Richard Jolly

Jimmy Glass

The title of an autobiography has rarely been more appropriate. Jimmy Glass's book was called *One-Hit Wonder*. But what a hit it was, and how wondrous. With a swing of his right boot, the goal-scoring goalkeeper saved Carlisle United's Football League status and catapulted himself into Cumbrian folklore.

The situation was bleak. In the final minute of added time, in the last game of the 1998-99 season, Carlisle were drawing 1-1 with Plymouth Argyle. Their 71-year stay in the Football League was at an end. "Everyone in the ground thought Carlisle were going to be relegated, myself included," said Glass.

Then Carlisle won a corner. They had hope, however slender. With nothing to lose, the manager Nigel Pearson waved Glass forward. And when Scott Dobie met Graham Anthony's corner with a header and Plymouth keeper James Dungey blocked, there was Glass, 100 yards from his own goal, to score the rebound. "It fell to me, wallop, goal, thank you very much," he recalled.

He barely had time to celebrate before he was buried beneath a mass of bodies. Jubilant Carlisle fans staged a pitch invasion, jumping on their new hero.

Few knew much about him. Glass was not even a Carlisle player. He had been borrowed from Swindon Town for the final three games of the season and, when no deal could be agreed, he went back there. He slipped from favour at the County Ground and fell out with the manager Jimmy Quinn. He played twice for Brentford and twice for Oxford United. Sixteen months after keeping Carlisle in the league, Glass played his final game.

He was never to return. He played non-league football, became an IT salesman and then a taxi driver, a normal life that was interrupted by reminders of an abnormal deed. In 2009, a Dubai radio station had a Jimmy Glass Day. Perhaps a brief career was damaged by his heroics. "Whereas I just wanted to be a goalkeeper, an anonymous goalkeeper that razzle-dazzled 'em with my skills, everywhere I went I carried the tag of Jimmy Glass, you know, 'That's the one that scored the goal'," he told the *Independent*.

Perhaps it hampered his chances of finding another club after left Swindon. Indeed, while he understudied Nigel Martyn at Crystal Palace and played behind an on-loan Rio Ferdinand for Bournemouth, he only had three seasons of regular first-team football in his career. If he was known for anything, it was for the 1998 Football League Trophy final when, playing for Bournemouth, he scored an own goal at Wembley. Then, incredibly, he achieved fleeting fame for putting the ball in the right net.

 ### 2 Roy Dwight

Some sportsmen have their 15 minutes of fame. Roy Dwight had 23 minutes in the sun before his career was plunged into the dark.

Briefly thrust into the spotlight, he was later eclipsed by a relative who never played professional football but nonetheless became a character in the sporting soap opera. When the 1959 FA Cup final began, Dwight was a promising winger for Nottingham Forest. It was a meeting of two underdogs at Wembley, Forest and Luton Town having both finished in the lower half of Division 1. Neither had won the FA Cup before, so there was a chance for someone to put his stamp on his club's history.

Dwight took his opportunity. After 10 minutes, Stewart Imlach – father of television presenter Gary – crossed and Dwight put Forest ahead. Four minutes later, Tommy Wilson added a second. Then disaster struck. Dwight broke his leg in a challenge with Luton's Brendan McNally. It ended his game. His career never recovered.

He was out for 10 months and, although he played on for Gravesend & Northfleet, Coventry and Millwall, he never scaled such heights again. But though the 1950s was a decade of injuries in FA Cup finals – the Manchester City goalkeeper Bert Trautmann had broken his neck in 1956

and his Manchester United counterpart Ray Wood fractured a cheekbone the following year – and a time before substitutions, Dwight's Forest held on.

Ten men were in effect reduced to nine for the final few minutes as Bill Whare struggled with cramp, but the depleted side did something Brian Clough never could in his golden reign and made Forest FA Cup winners.

It was a one-off for them and for Dwight, but his family were not finished in football. Roy's cousin Reg lacked his sporting talent but went on to become the owner and chairman of a club, in Watford, who provided one of the surprise success stories of the 1980s. But the younger Dwight was better known by the stage name he adopted in his musical career: Elton John.

 ### 3 Roy Essandoh

The nickname denoted a certain time in technology. Perhaps today he would have been 'the Twitter scorer' or 'the Instagram attacker'. In the days before social media, Roy Essandoh was 'the Teletext striker', the man who went down in football folklore for being signed because of an article that appeared in blockish type on television screens and who scored an injury-time winner for the lower-league underdogs in an FA Cup quarter-final.

Essandoh's rapid rise was remarkable. Too remarkable, Essandoh subsequently said, admitting that the legend had overtaken the facts. "The version everyone knows makes for a better story," the forward told *Footy Matters* wryly in 2011.

But however it is told, his tale is unique – certainly in the modern game, perhaps ever.

While Wycombe Wanderers, a mid-table third-flight club, embarked on an FA Cup run in 2001, their forwards acquired injury after injury. High-profile attempts to get Ian Wright or Gianluca Vialli out of retirement failed and an article on the club's website referred to manager Lawrie Sanchez's search for a striker. On Teletext, that was interpreted as an appeal for attackers to present themselves.

Actually, Essandoh said, he had already been signed until the end of the season after his agent had alerted Sanchez to his availability. "It seemed people put two and two together and made five," Essandoh added.

However he reached Wycombe, he was an unlikely candidate for stardom: born in Belfast and brought up in Ghana, he had played in Scotland and Finland. He had appeared twice for Wanderers when they visited high-flying Leicester City in the FA Cup.

With a quarter of an hour remaining, Sanchez sent for Essandoh. Then the manager himself departed, sent from the dugout to watch the drama unfold on a Filbert Street monitor, a drenched figure in a raincoat seeing a surreal ending. In the 92nd minute, Jamie Bates headed the ball across the box and, rising above the defence, Essandoh nodded in. Then, in a pointless piece of pedantry by referee Steve Bennett, the midfielder Steve Brown was sent off for his celebrations. Despite that, Wycombe held on.

But lightning did not strike twice. Essandoh got 34 minutes as a semi-final substitute against Liverpool, without making the same impact. Indeed, he never scored again for Wycombe. He never scored in the Football League either, instead taking a tour of the semi-professional game with Barnet, Cambridge City, Bishop's Stortford, Billericay, Grays Athletic, Gravesend & Northfleet, Kettering, St Neots, Braintree and Bury Town. Wycombe proved the seventh of eighteen clubs he represented in a peripatetic career. But even if Essandoh was not found on Teletext, he went on to make headlines, in newspapers, on radio and even, when it still existed, on Ceefax.

 Steve Morrow

Steve Morrow looked like his manager George Graham, played like Arsenal's many other defensive midfielders of the early 1990s and became the answer to a pub quiz question.

His moment of glory led to a piece of trivia: he is the only Cup winner to collect his medal before a final, the result of a celebration gone horribly wrong.

The 1993 League Cup final against Sheffield Wednesday was level at 1-1 when Paul Merson, with a little inadvertent assistance from Carlton Palmer, set up Morrow for the winner. It was his first Arsenal goal – there were only two more in the rest of his Gunners career – and after the final whistle went, he ran to Tony Adams. The Arsenal captain attempted to lift up the goalscorer. Instead, Morrow tumbled over his shoulder, landing awkwardly and breaking his arm. Rather than climbing Wembley's 39 steps, he was taken to hospital.

"The whole thing has devalued the day for us," Graham said after the game. "Steve had an excellent game, nullifying John Sheridan, and what has happened to him spoiled everything for me, and all the players."

So Morrow's journey to the Royal Box was postponed. But 1993 was a year of two finals between Arsenal and Wednesday and while the injured Northern Irishman missed the FA Cup meeting, he was at least able to pick up his League Cup medal before kick-off.

Arsenal won in a replay to complete a Cup double but while Morrow recovered physically, his career did not. He broke through at a particular point in Arsenal's history: the title-winning sides of 1989 and 1991 were famously sound defensively but possessed attacking options.

The latter-period Graham teams became disproportionately reliant on Ian Wright for goals – he delivered thirty in 1992-93, while Kevin Campbell, with nine, was Arsenal's second highest scorer – and featured fewer flair players, with Anders Limpar figuring less in the starting XI. Instead the midfield was staffed by seemingly interchangeable defensive-minded players: Ian Selley, David Hillier and Morrow, who could also operate as a right-back or central defender.

Indeed, Morrow lined up alongside Selley in the centre of the pitch in the 1994 Cup Winners' Cup final victory over Parma, but it was one of just 13 appearances that season. After Graham was succeeded by

Bruce Rioch and then Arsène Wenger, he dropped out of the reckoning altogether. Morrow left Arsenal in the summer Emmanuel Petit arrived, completing a partnership with Patrick Vieira and a midfield upgrade.

The Northern Irishman eventually joined QPR but, after being loaned to Peterborough, was released on a free transfer. Unable to find a club in England, the former minor character in the Arsenal drama joined Dallas Burn. He later managed the Major League Soccer club before becoming Arsenal's international partnerships performance supervisor. Wembley winner was a rather simpler title in a day when Arsenal's team was packed with graduates of their youth system, like Morrow, and an international partnership involved passing to the Swedish winger Limpar. Morrow was one of the Brits swept aside by Arsenal's foreign invasion but only after he had a unique role in two Cup finals in the same season.

5 Roger Osborne

Perhaps it was just as well that Roger Osborne only scored one FA Cup-winning goal given what a shock to the system it was for the Ipswich Town midfielder.

Because it is not merely his 1978 strike – a left-footed shot after the Arsenal defender Willie Young failed to clear David Geddis's cross – that is memorable. It was the celebration. An overcome Osborne fainted. Smelling salts were required to bring him around and the manager Bobby Robson promptly substituted him.

Twelve minutes later, the referee Derek Nippard blew the final whistle and

Ipswich, for the only time in their history, were FA Cup winners. In many ways Osborne was a fitting hero for both the club – born in the Suffolk village of Otley, he was a local – and the times. The 1970s was a decade where some of the least likely lads proved to be the match-winners.

And there was nothing obvious about Osborne deciding the destination of the trophy. Missed by Ipswich's scouts as a boy, he did not make his debut for them until he was 23, having been signed from Grundisburgh. After a slow start, he went on to establish himself in Robson's midfield as Ipswich twice finished third in Division 1. But the 1978 campaign progressed rather less smoothly and he was dropped for Colin Viljoen the week before the FA Cup final. Ipswich's 6-1 defeat to Aston Villa, with Viljoen in the side and without Osborne, prompted a rethink by Robson.

Yet Osborne's finest moment was the beginning of the end for him. After winning his first major trophy, Robson grew more ambitious. His horizons broadened and his style of play became more expansive as he signed the Dutch duo of Arnold Mühren and Frans Thijssen to add flair to his midfield. Osborne was one of those to make way and by the time Ipswich won the Uefa Cup in 1981, their Wembley winner had faded from the reckoning.

He went on loan to Detroit Express, but his career wound down in East Anglia, at Colchester United, Sudbury, Braintree and Felixstowe. It is not a fate that is likely to await more recent FA Cup final heroes. Nor is driving a lorry or managing a sports centre, two of the jobs Osborne has done after his retirement from football. Still, such a taste of everyday life

should not have been exciting enough to make him faint again.

 Tony Parks

Depending upon your perspective, being the reserve goalkeeper is either the easiest or the hardest job in football. When the first choice is a player of the quality of Ray Clemence, who played more than 1,000 games in his career, being his understudy seemed a guarantee of a watching brief. But his deputy emerged from the shadows and was propelled into the limelight the last time Tottenham won a European trophy. An unknown 21 year old from Hackney was the hero.

Clemence had suffered a rare injury in 1984, a finger problem that meant Parks got his chance. After excelling against Hajduk Split in the Uefa Cup semi-final, the manager Keith Burkinshaw kept faith with Parks in the final. For once, a fit-again Clemence was on the bench. So was a semi-fit Ossie Ardiles. The injured Glenn Hoddle was absent altogether. Stripped of their stars, Spurs had a more workman-like look. They were underdogs.

And after the first leg against Anderlecht was drawn 1-1, Graham Roberts's second-leg equaliser took the tie to penalty kicks. It was time for Parks. "He was always a great penalty saver, even in training," Roberts recalled. Parks flung himself to his left to save the first, taken by the future Denmark manager Morten Olsen. He dived the same way for each of Anderlecht's next three penalties. All went in.

Then, after Danny Thomas had missed the chance to win it for Spurs, Parks made the decisive save in the shootout. The Belgians' fifth spot-kick was taken by Arnór Guðjohnsen, father of the future Chelsea and Barcelona forward Eiður. It was a well-struck penalty but Parks dived to his right to make a superb save before sprinting off in celebration.

"If the gates had been open 10 minutes before [the end] as they were in a league game, I'd have been at Seven Sisters in about 35 seconds," Parks said later. "Luckily enough, I just remember Ray Clemence clothes-lining me as I ran past him."

His reward was to be demoted to third-choice goalkeeper when Bobby Mimms joined as back-up to Clemence. Parks never did become the regular at White Hart Lane and became the definition of a journeyman, appearing for Oxford, Gillingham, Brentford, QPR, Fulham, West Ham, Stoke, Falkirk, Blackpool, Burnley, Doncaster, Barrow, Scarborough and Halifax, without staying anywhere for long before eventually returning to Tottenham as goalkeeping coach in 2008 and, more recently, moving on to Aston Villa.

"I reached my Everest at the age of 21," he said many years later. But what a peak it was. And while Tottenham have had plenty of world-class talents since, the reality is that the last man to win them a European trophy was a second-string shot-stopper who would never have played if Clemence had stayed fit.

 ### 7 Mike Trebilcock

1966 was a great year for English attackers. Two months before Geoff Hurst's unforgettable treble at Wembley, another forward struck twice beneath

the Twin Towers to win a trophy. But while Hurst earned fame everlasting, Mike Trebilcock was quickly forgotten – or he was outside Merseyside, anyway. A brief Everton career featured a great high for a young man catapulted into the limelight.

Five months earlier, Trebilcock had been a Plymouth player. But he had appeared in Everton's FA Cup semi-final win over Manchester United and when the manager Harry Catterick decided Fred Pickering was not fully for the final, he resisted the temptation to move Jimmy Gabriel further forward and instead picked the untried Trebilcock.

It did not seem Catterick's finest decision. "You can imagine how I felt," Trebilcock told Backpass in 2010. "The boss drops the England centre-forward, puts me in the team, we're 2-0 down, and I've not had a kick for an hour. But in the blink of an eye, everything changed." Trebilcock sprung to life with two goals in five minutes. Derek Temple completed the comeback to make Everton FA Cup winners for the first time since the days of Dixie Dean. "That was my greatest moment," said Catterick, ranking his FA Cup win above his two league titles. It was Trebilcock's, too. Conforming to cup cliché, he had a boyhood obsession with Roy of the Rovers. This was almost a script suitable for his fictional idol.

"It all went according to my dreams," he added. "I always knew I'd play for a top club, then play in an FA Cup final, then score the winning goal. I didn't get the winning goal, but I got the next best thing: I scored twice, then I helped another young player score the winner."

Watched by John Lennon and Paul McCartney, two Liverpudlian day-trippers with a ticket to Wembley, Everton had ensured Merseyside was England's football and musical capital. Liverpool had already won Division 1.

But Trebilcock's stint at the top of the charts was brief. Pickering returned, a young Joe Royle emerged and Temple, Jimmy Husband and Alex Young remained key components of Catterick's side. The Wembley hero spent more time on the sidelines. He only scored three league goals in an Everton career that spanned a mere 13 games before moving on to Portsmouth and then back to his native south-west at Torquay. The Cornishman, the youngest of 14 children, had begun at non-league Tavistock before joining Plymouth. There, he had to borrow £5 to get the train to Crewe so he could sign for Everton.

And, at an age when others are at the peak of his footballing powers, he made a rather longer journey. At just 29, he emigrated to Australia, where he still lives. He could scarcely be further away from the scene of his greatest day but in May 1966 Trebilcock and Wembley were, like Lennon and McCartney, in perfect harmony.

 8 Mickey Evans

The winners of the Premier League Player of the Month award tend to be distinguished. There are World Cup and Champions League winners, record signings and prolific scorers and players who meet even the strictest test of greatness.

Then, every now and then, comes an anomaly, a player who stands out precisely because he is so different from the other exalted individuals on

an illustrious list. Alex Manninger, Anton Ferdinand, Johan Elmander and Adam Le Fondre are such occasional oddities. But none, surely, is as unlikely as the man honoured for his exploits in April 1997.

Mickey Evans was a striker who only ever scored four Premier League goals. They all came within a 15-day period. They made a huge impact. Southampton were engaged in their annual struggle to stay up when Graeme Souness signed Evans from Plymouth. He failed to score in his first five games and was on the bench when they visited their relegation rivals Nottingham Forest on April 5.

With a quarter of an hour remaining, he came on for Matt Le Tissier. Two goals in three minutes, sandwiching a Stuart Pearce penalty, clinched a 3-1 win. The following week Southampton hosted West Ham, another team in danger of the drop. Evans opened the scoring in a 2-0 victory. Seven days later, they faced Coventry who, needless to say, were not safe themselves. Evans netted again, in a 2-2 draw. Southampton, who had propped up the table before the Forest game, clambered out of the bottom three.

They remained a Premier League club, but Evans did not remain a top-flight player. Souness left Saints that summer. His replacement, Dave Jones, preferred to use Kevin Davies, whose arrival from Chesterfield was set up by Souness, and his own buy David Hirst and sold the award-winner to West Brom. Evans only scored six Division 1 goals before returning to his native Plymouth, where he made his name and for whom, spread over two spells, 73 of his 88 league goals came, the vast majority in the bottom two divisions of the Football League. Evans was capped once by the Republic of Ireland, but he was a Devonian, down to a rustic look that made him a cult hero at Southampton. Certainly there was no sheen of class to his game.

Perhaps only a manager of such strong belief in his opinions and with such a disdain for conventional wisdom as Souness could have signed Evans. His recruitment throughout his career was eclectic, ranging from the inspired to the disastrous. During his sole season at Southampton, he signed Richard Dryden from Exeter who, like Evans, discovered Souness was the only manager to give him regular top-flight football, at times in a back three featuring the attacking midfielder Neil Maddison. The Scot introduced Egil Østenstad, an underrated goalscorer, and Eyal Berkovic, a magical talent. Together with Le Tissier, they had orchestrated the famous 6-3 defeat of Manchester United.

Each possessed far more ability than Evans but he added another ingredient to the attack. Bustling around with more enthusiasm than finesse, the target man's rough-and-ready approach proved what Southampton needed. If he was an incongruous sight alongside Le Tissier and Berkovic, he was still more so in the list of the division's men of the month. He was preceded by Juninho and succeeded by Dennis Bergkamp, two of the first great wave of inventive imports. In contrast, Evans represented a throwback to the days when clubs were likelier to gamble on unassuming workhorses from the lower leagues. Ⓑ

Blizzard Books

Johnny Cook: The Impossible Job

Iain Macintosh

Attention Blizzard fans, we now do books!

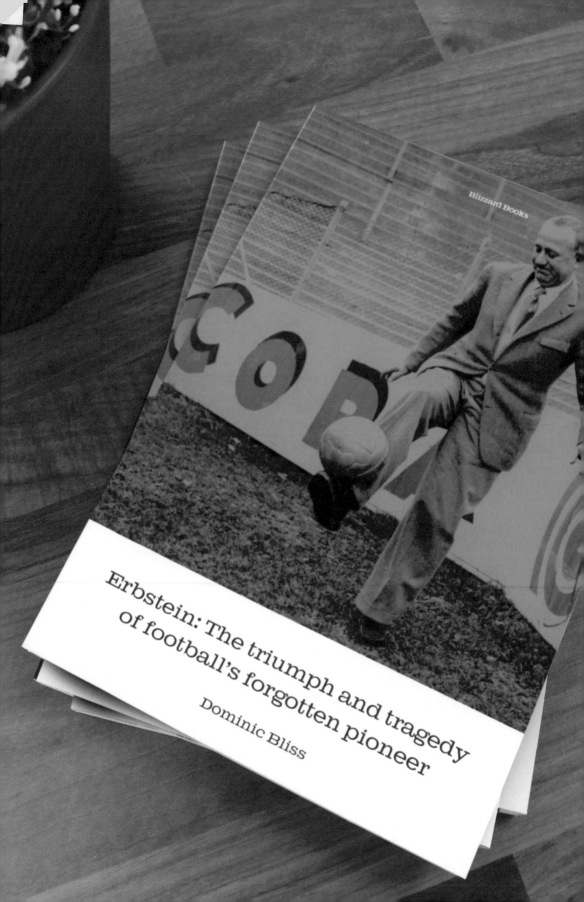

Erbstein: The triumph and tragedy
of football's forgotten pioneer

Dominic Bliss

THE BLIZZARD BY GOALSOUL

01

02

03

04

01 . 02 . 03
GOALS ARE OVERRATED

04
THE HARMONY OF THE SPHERE

05
COMPARING APPLE WITH ORANJE

06
THE BICYCLE THIEF

07
DOLPHINS ARE B@#!&*DS

08
THE SECONDS OF THE GREATS
LAST LONGER

05

06

07

08

The Blizzard by goalsoul partnership is a commitment to style and substance in equal measure. Our stunning and original story-inspired, graphic tees look and feel great. Lovingly hand screen-printed on 100% combed-cotton and shrink-resistant fabric — you can be sure of the highest possible quality, durability and wearability. Exclusively available online from www.theblizzard.co.uk and www.goalsoul.net

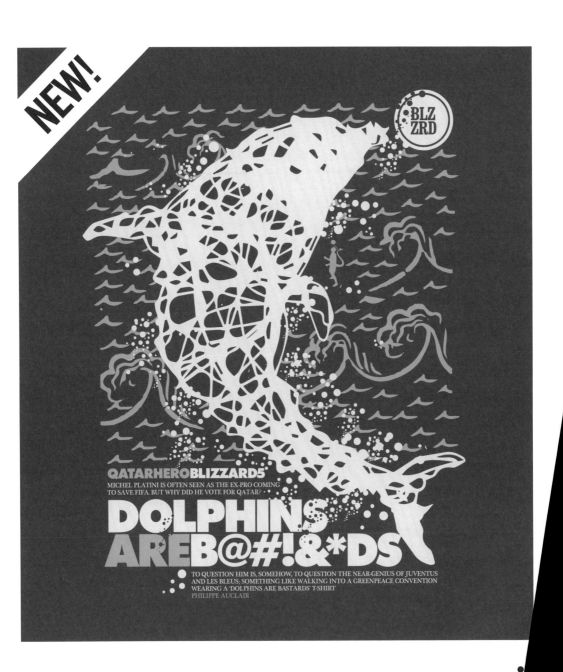

Contributors

The Blizzard, Issue Nineteen

Paul Brown is a half-Finnish freelance sports journalist and long-suffering Evertonian on the London football beat. Currently found most often in the *Daily Star*. Twitter: **@pbsportswriter**

Jamil Chade has been the European correspondent for the Brazilian daily *O Estado de S. Paulo* since 2000. He has written four books and was one of the researchers of the Truth Commission established by the government in Brazil to investigate the crimes committed during the military dictatorship.

Dermot Corrigan is an Irish sportswriter who lives in Madrid and covers Spanish football for publications including ESPN, the *Irish Examiner* and *When Saturday Comes*. He's also the host of the podcast Covering Fútbol. Twitter: **@dermotmcorrigan**

Charles Ducksbury is an English football writer based in Sheffield. He contributes to PN, CNN and *FourFourTwo*.

ert **Fryer** is a freelance journalist and of BrasilGlobalTour.com. He has on South American football for of Fox Sports, the *Guardian*, the , Goal, ESPN and *8by8*. Twitter: .Fryer

a British freelance journalist harest where he covers the e likes of the *Guardian*, the s and the *Christian Science* others. Twitter: **@KitGillet**

Maciej Iwanski is a football presenter and commentator for TVP. He is Polish member of the Fifa Ballon d'Or jury. Twitter: **@iwanskimaciej**

Richard Jolly is a football journalist for ESPN, the *National*, the *Guardian*, the *Observer*, the *Straits Times*, the *Sunday Express*, Eurosport and Goal. He has written for 14 British national daily or Sunday newspapers. Twitter: **@RichJolly**

Alex Keble is a freelance journalist who writes for *FourFourTwo*, the Independent and Squawka, amongst others. Website: www.alexkeble.tk. Twitter: **@alexkeble**

Felix Lill is a German freelance journalist who works as an author for *Die Zeit*, *Die Presse*, *Der Spiegel*, *Neue Zürcher Zeitung*, *Tagesspiegel*, *Zeit Online* and others. He was awarded the Austrian Sports Journalism Award in 2010, 2011 and 2012. He was awarded the Austrian OEZIV Media Prize 2012.

Peter Linden has written about Austrian football since 1969. He works for the daily *Kronen-Zeitung* and has covered every World Cup since 1974.

Iain Macintosh is a reporter for ESPNFC and the editor of The Set Pieces. He is a regular on the *Guardian*'s Football Weekly podcast and has published eight books, the latest of which is *The Football Manager Guide to Football Management*. Twitter: **@iainmacintosh**

Przemek Niciejewski is a Polish football photographer specialising in the culture of the game. Twitter: **@niciejewski1**

Vladimir Novak is a freelance sports journalist based in Belgrade. He writes for *World Soccer*, *Titan Sports* (China) and *World Soccer Digest* (Japan), reports for SID (Sport Informations Dienst) and works as producer for Pitch International Fifa Football. Twitter: **@vnovak13**

Arthur O'Dea is a second-year doctoral student of American Literature in Dublin City University. **@ArthurJamesOD**

Ally Palmer is an award-winning editorial designer based in Edinburgh. His company Palmer Watson have been responsible for newspaper redesigns around the world. He also runs the music review aggregator AnyDecentMusic and is a life-long Ayr United supporter. Twitter: **@HonestManAlly**

Harry Pearson is the author of *The Far Corner*. His blog about north-east football, The First Thirty Years Are The Worst, is unaccountably popular in Ukraine. This season he has paid an average £1.36 per goal in the Ebac Northern League, which is a few pence more than his friend Gary. Not that it's a competition, or anything. Twitter: **@camsell59**

Gunnar Persson is a Swedish author and editor specialising in football. He has written a biography of Lennart 'Nacka' Skoglund as well as club histories on *Hakoah Vienna, IFK Norrköping, Motala AIF and Hammarby IF*. His history of Serie A was published this year.

Alex Preston is the award-winning author of three novels: *This Bleeding City, The Revelations and In Love and War*. He teaches Creative Writing at the University of Kent and *Guardian* Masterclasses. He is Contributing Editor of *Town & Country* Magazine and writes for *Harper's Bazaar* and *Guardian Long Reads* as well as monthly fiction reviews for the *Observer*. He is the youngest member of the Authors XI cricket team and the oldest footballer in the West London Sunday League. Twitter: **@ahmpreston**

Javier Sauras is a nomadic journalist and photographer who has been wandering from Asia to Latin America during the last four years. He has written about Japan, the Philippines, Spain, China, UK and Bolivia. He is still on the road. Twitter: **@jsauras**

Craig Smith is a songwriter, community manager, event organiser and poet. His most recent novel is called *Super 8*, published by Kennedy and Boyd. Twitter: **@smithylad**.

Jonathan Wilson is the author of *Inverting the Pyramid*. He writes for the *Guardian*, *World Soccer,* Fox and *Sports Illustrated*. He is writing a book on the history of Argentinian football. Twitter: **@jonawils**

Blizzard **Subscriptions**

Subscribe to the print version of The Blizzard, *be the first to receive new issues, get exclusive Blizzard offers and access digital versions of all back-issues FREE*

Subscription Options

Set Price for Four Issues

Get a four-issue subscription to *The Blizzard* — for you or as a gift — for a flat fee including postage and packing (P&P):

UK:	£35
Europe:	£45
Non-Euorpe:	£55

Recurring Pay-What-You-Like

Set up a quarterly recurring payment for each edition of *The Blizzard*. The recommended retail price (RRP) is £12, but pay what you like, subject to a minimum fee of £6 plus P&P.

See www.theblizzard.co.uk for more

Digital Subscriptions

If the cost of postage is prohibitive, or you just want an excuse to use your new iPad or Kindle, you can set up a subscription to digital versions of The Blizzard for just £3 per issue.

See *www.theblizzard.co.uk* for more

Information for Existing Subscribers

The Blizzard is a quarterly publication from a cooperative of top class football journalists and authors from across the globe, enjoying the space and freedom to write about the football stories that matter to them.

Free Digital Downloads for *Blizzard* Subscribers

Whether you have taken advantage of our set price or pay-what-you-like offer, for the duration of your subscription to *The Blizzard* you are entitled to download every issue FREE.

See www.theblizzard.co.uk for more

We very much value the commitment of our print subscribers and have a policy to make available new issues, special offers and other limited access events and benefits to print subscribers first.

About *The Blizzard*

Distribution & Back Issues
Contact Information
About Issue Nineteen

Buy *The Blizzard*

We want as many readers as possible for *The Blizzard*. We therefore operate as far as we are able on a pay-what-you-like basis for digital and print versions.

Digital Version (Current & Back Issues)

All issues of *The Blizzard* are available to download for Kindle, Android, iOS and PC/Mac at: *www.theblizzard.co.uk*.

- *RRP: £3*
- *Pay-what-you-like minimum: £0.01*

Printed Version (Current & Back Issues)

Purchase a physical copy of *The Blizzard* in all its luxurious, tactile, sensual glory at: *www.theblizzard.co.uk*. If you haven't felt our rough textured cover-varnish and smelled the inner genius, you haven't properly experienced its awesome true form. Read it, or leave it on your coffee table to wow visitors.

- *RRP: £12 (+P&P)*
- *Pay-what-you-like min: £6 (+P&P)*

Contact *The Blizzard*

All advertising, sales, press and business communication should be addressed to the Central Publishing Office:

The Blizzard
Ashmore Villa,
1, Ashmore Terrace,
Stockton Road,
Sunderland,
SR2 7DE

Email: info@theblizzard.co.uk
Telephone: +44 (0) 191 543 8785
Website: www.theblizzard.co.uk
Facebook: www.facebook.com/blzzrd
Twitter: @blzzrd

About Issue Nineteen

Editor Jonathan Wilson
Publisher The Blizzard Media Ltd
www.theblizzard.co.uk
Design Daykin & Storey
www.daykinandstorey.co.uk

Copyright

All content is ©Copyright The Blizzard Media Ltd and may not be reproduced without explicit consent. Thanks to Jeanette G Sturis at the Kingsley Motel, Manjimup, for kind use of Warren Walker's original sketches of Dog.

THE FOOTBALL SUPPORTERS' FEDERATION

The Football Supporters' Federation
By Fans, For Fans

 **INFORMING**

 **SUPPORTING**

 **CAMPAIGNING**

- www.fsf.org.uk
- Free Lions Magazine
- The Football Supporter Magazine

- Legal Advice and Support
- International Fans' Embassies
- Case Work and Consumer Advice

- Local Campaigns
- National Representation
- Football Supporters Europe

Join the fsf today for FREE visit: www.fsf.org.uk